Revise the Anthology
For
GCSE English Literature

2000 – 2003

Tony Childs
Principal Examiner

Heinemann Educational Publishers
Halley Court, Jordan Hill, Oxford OX2 8EJ
A division of Reed Educational and Professional Publishing Ltd

OXFORD BLANTYRE CHICAGO PORTSMOUTH NH (USA)
MELBOURNE AUCKLAND IBADAN GABORONE JOHANNESBURG

First published 1999

03 02 01
10 9 8 7 6 5 4

ISBN 0 435 10127 7

Designed and produced by 320 Design
Cover illustration by Arlene Adams
Printed and bound in the UK by Biddles Ltd.

Acknowledgements

The publishers would like to thank the following for permission to
reproduce photographs on the pages noted: Faber & Faber/Rollie McKenna
p18; Henry Slesar p21; HarperCollins Children's Books p24; HarperCollins
(Trade Division) p27; Little Brown & Co. (UK) p31; Penguin UK p34; Irish
Times/Macmillan Publishers Ltd p37.

Contents

About this book

This book is for GCSE students who are going to sit the NEAB examination in English Literature, and who are going to use the NEAB **Anthology** to respond to questions on prose or poetry, or both.

The book acts as a revision guide and as a self-study aid. Most of you are likely to have studied the **Anthology** material in class, with your teachers. Working through the relevant sections in this book will help to consolidate the work done in class, and to provide a springboard for tackling the examination itself with confidence. Some of you, for one reason or another, may be working independently or at home. You can use this book to select the best sections to study, and to prepare thoroughly for the examination.

The main sections of the book are designed to take you through all the short stories and poems in the English Literature **Anthology**. Following the questions and suggestions carefully will help you to explore and understand the content and language of the pieces. Applying purposeful annotation will be useful in revision and in the examination itself. How to do this practically is shown in each of the sections.

Each short story and each poetry cluster is followed by sample questions for Foundation and Higher Tier candidates. They are written in the same style and at the same level as the questions in the NEAB examinations. There are also some suggestions about possible points of comparison at the end of the prose section and after each poetry cluster.

The book also outlines how the **Anthology** fits into the English Literature course, indicates what examiners are looking for In your answers, and gives advice on how to revise and how to tackle the examination, including some suggestions about how you might structure and detail responses to a sample question on both prose and poetry. At the back of the book there are sample answers to examination questions, with an examiner's comments showing how the answers would be assessed.

How the English Literature Anthology fits into the course

The NEAB GCSE English Literature course is assessed through a terminal examination, which counts for 70%, and coursework, which counts for 30%, of the final mark.

In the examination, there are two sections, A and B. Section A has questions based on twentieth-century prose; Section B has questions on pre-twentieth-century and twentieth-century poetry. You have to answer one question from each section.

For each section, there is a choice of texts in the syllabus. The prose section in the English Literature **Anthology** is one of the choices in Section A; the poetry section in the English Literature **Anthology** is one of the choices in Section B. So, you might be doing one part of the **Anthology** for the examination, or both, or neither. It depends on what you or your teachers have chosen. The texts are common to both tiers of entry, so whether you are entered for Foundation Tier or Higher Tier makes no difference to the study of the texts themselves.

Whichever texts you are studying, you will be offered a choice of two questions on each of them. This book gives you some advice on choosing questions in the section on 'Preparing for the examination' on page 13.

Prose texts from the **Anthology** can also be used in the Wide Reading coursework assignment. If you are doing this, the questions on the short stories will help you come to grips with the content and style of the stories you are using.

The Assessment Objectives

The Assessment Objectives for any examination syllabus show what candidates have to do in their examinations for that syllabus. Examiners have to decide how well individual candidates have fulfilled these objectives in their examination performance, and give marks accordingly.

Here are the Assessment Objectives for GCSE English Literature. Candidates must demonstrate their ability to:

1 **Respond to texts critically, sensitively and in detail, selecting suitable ways to convey their response, using textual evidence as appropriate.**

   This simply means that you have to show that you can think about your texts, not just repeat what they say, and that you should be able to support what you have to say about the texts with some evidence, through quotations or other means of showing your knowledge. The more sensitive, detailed and organized you can be in your response, the better.

2 **Explore how language, structure and forms contribute to the meanings of texts, considering different approaches to texts and alternative interpretations.**

   This emphasizes that you should be able to write not just about *what* a text means, but *how* it is written; about writers' methods and devices, and the ways in which a writer's style can support and add to what he or she has to say. Also, you should be able to think about the same words or texts having a range of possible meanings, rather than just one.

3 **Explore relationships and comparisons within and between texts, selecting and evaluating relevant material.**

   Comparison – how we understand one thing through comparing it to another – is at the heart of literature in all sorts of ways. Working out 'comparisons within texts' has much to do with writers' devices, and so is connected to the second Assessment Objective above. The questions on the **Anthology** in the examination will ask you to make 'comparisons between texts' – to compare one short story with another, or several poems with each other, in what they say and how they say it. To do this, you have to choose the right material to look at and assess.

4   **Show an understanding of literary tradition and appreciation of social and historical influences and cultural contexts.**

In terms of the **Anthology**, you only need to think about this Assessment Objective if you are doing the poetry section for the examination. Each cluster of poems contains two written before 1900, and you have to choose at least one of these to write about. Questions may invite you to show your knowledge of social, historical or cultural contexts; of how language is different because of these issues, for instance, or how attitudes can be affected by cultural experience. Always remember, though, that what you write must be linked clearly to the poems themselves. Don't spend time writing about the background to a poem rather than the poem itself.

What the examiners will expect to see

The questions on the examination paper will be designed to test how well the candidates can fulfil the Assessment Objectives through writing about their chosen texts in response to the questions. So what will examiners expect to see?

Simply, they will want to see that you know your texts, and can think about them. *Knowing your texts* means not only being familiar with the details, but also understanding what they mean (in your view) and how they're written, and being able to move around them confidently to support what you have to say, without necessarily having to look them up all the time!

Thinking about your texts means showing your opinions and understanding of the texts in response to the questions that you have been asked. This may seem very obvious – but often candidates try to write down everything they know about a text, rather than answering the question, hoping that some of it will be relevant. This isn't the right way to go about it, just as telling the story isn't the right way to go about it. That's why learning an 'answer' before you go into the exam is never the right thing to do – after all, you don't know what the question will be! Go into the exam knowing your texts, and respond directly to the questions.

How to use this book to help you

In order to approach your exams with confidence, you need to understand *what* the writers of the pieces you have studied are saying, and *how* they say it. Then you need to be able to draw on that knowledge in the examination to answer the questions quickly and effectively. Because this is an 'open book' examination – that is to say, you can take your texts in with you, and they can be annotated – you can use them to remind you of some of the important points about each piece.

1 Approaching the texts through the questions

Where it's helpful to know something about an author in order to understand a story or poem better, or to know the meanings of some of the words (if they are archaic, for instance, or belong to a particular dialect), this information has been given at the start of the section on that particular story or poem. Generally, however, the emphasis is on you finding out about the piece yourself through a series of structured questions.

Questions

Before you begin working through the questions, you should always read through the piece once, to get a feel for it; it's vital to do this without any preconceptions, so that you begin to form your own response to it. If you're using the book as a revision aid, you should still do this, to remind yourself of the text.

Now start working through the questions. If you like, you can make notes in a separate notebook or on paper as you go; but simply thinking through the questions may well be enough, as long as you use annotation sensibly, as indicated below. The questions are designed to take you through the pieces in logical steps, getting you to think about what the writers are saying and how they are saying it. Sometimes 'logical' means going through the piece chronologically, from beginning to end, looking for things on the way, and seeing the developing structure; sometimes you may be asked to take an overall view from the start.

Final thoughts

This section is important. It nearly always asks you to read the piece again, and poses a final, usually general, question. It's important because, having worked through the questions, your initial response may well have been modified in some way; a further reading will confirm what you have observed about the piece as a whole, and may lead to some fresh thoughts in the light of what you've learnt.

2 Annotation

The instructions in the NEAB syllabus about annotation read as follows:

Candidates' copies of the **Anthology** *may be annotated. Annotation means brief handwritten marginal notes, underlinings, highlightings, and vertical lines in the margin. Additional notes on loose, interleaved sheets of paper and/or prepared answers are not permitted.*

What you *can't* do should be quite clear; another way of thinking about it might be that you can't bring in lots of continuous writing. It wouldn't help you anyway (remember that you won't know the questions before you go in), and if you attempt to do so, you may well be disqualified from the examination. So what *can* you do, and what is the best way to use annotation to help you in the exam, and before it?

If you've been working on these materials in class, you may already have made some annotations, which is fine – the more you work on the texts the better! The questions in this book simply offer you some more ideas.

Several of the questions on each piece may ask you to look for and underline certain words and phrases. This is a way of highlighting issues about meaning or style which may be important in looking at the text, and once you've done it, when you come back to look at the piece again, you already know that these words are important. If there is more than one issue highlighted by underlining (they'll be in separate questions), then you need to devise a key for knowing why these are important, and what the difference is; for instance, you could use blue to underline the verbs you've been asked to pick out, and red for the rhyming words, with a key at the bottom of the page.

Similarly, some questions will suggest that you 'mark' certain features. Devise your own way of doing this; it might be in symbols or notes alongside or above the line or the word. Most of the questions ask you to look for something, or to think about something – when you come to write an answer, you may find it useful to have indicated this somewhere on the page, so that you'll remember it when you come back to it, either in revision or in the examination. Remember that what you're applying are *brief handwritten marginal notes, underlinings, highlightings, and vertical lines in the margin.*

3 Points of comparison

After the prose section, and after each poetry cluster in this book, you'll find notes on the ways in which the stories, or the poems in the cluster, might be compared. The exam question will ask you to compare texts, so it's useful and important to start thinking along these lines. Of course, the suggestions here are not the only ones. It's not possible to note down *every* way of looking at every possible combination of poems or stories, and anyway you don't know the questions before you go into the exam. It's better to think of these suggestions as examples of *how* you might compare the poems or stories.

4 Sample structures

At the end of the prose section and at the end of the poetry section, you'll find examples of how a response to a particular question might be structured and detailed. Again, these are only suggestions – there are all sorts of ways of structuring responses, and you don't know the questions – but they will show you a method of organizing your ideas so that you can show off your knowledge effectively.

5 The practice examination questions

Each short story and each poetry cluster Is followed by practice examination questions, one for each tier. At the back of the book you will also find some sample examination answers, each with an examiner's commentary.

Whether or not you actually try answering them (and if you do, the best thing is to give yourself an hour to do one, as you will in the exam itself), you should look at these questions very carefully to see what sort of thing you will be expected to do. The question type and format are exactly the same as you will face in the examination.

Even if you don't answer the questions in full, it will help you to make essay plans for each question. Decide which poems you would concentrate on in your answer and what you would say about each poem. Decide how you would respond to each of the bullet points.

Preparing for the examination

1 Revision

The texts

The most important thing to do is simply to re-read the texts themselves. This will help to make you more familiar with the details of each, so you don't need to look things up all the time during the exam – but it will also help you to find new things as well. Even if you're in the last week before the examination, you should aim to find the time to read all your chosen texts at least twice, looking at the points you've picked up before, and read them with a fresh eye as well.

Using this book

If you're using this book as a revision aid you may find that the questions seem to take you in a different direction from the one you took with your teachers. Don't worry about this! What the examiner is interested in is what *you* think and the more different ways you look at a text, the more likely it is that you will come to a firm view of what *you* think about it. *What is important is that you can argue for your point of view, drawing on the text for evidence.*

If you are using this book as a self-study guide, you will probably need to make some choices before you start your final revision. The exam questions on the short stories are comparative, so it's as well to get to know them all, to give yourself the widest possible range to answer from. The questions on poetry are for the most part divided into questions on individual clusters of poems. You can get away with just studying closely one group of poems; if you do two, you'll give yourself more choice in the examination, and the opportunity of tackling a cross-cluster question (see opposite); but it's probably not necessary to look at all five clusters in great detail. If you use this book sensibly in preparation, you'll probably come to a decision quite easily as to which groups to concentrate on in your final revision, that is, those that you find most interesting as groups, and can write about most effectively.

Comparing stories and poems

All the exam questions will ask you to compare texts – one story with another or several poems together. It's important to think about this when revising too. The questions here on the stories and poems are designed to get you to think about those individual texts, because there are any number of different ways in which they might be 'paired', and after all, knowing the texts is the most important thing. Nevertheless, the better you get to know them, the more likely you are to see similarities and differences between them, both in content and style, and you should consciously look for these comparisons in the late stages of revision. Some of the stories might seem to 'fit' together more obviously – the 'points of comparison' sections should help to identify some of these – *but you should be prepared for any combination.*

Poetry

There are two special things to notice about the exam questions on poetry. The first is that *you must refer to at least one pre-twentieth-century poem* in your answer, whichever question you choose. The pre-twentieth-century poems are always indicated in the question and in the **Anthology** itself. The second is that, after all the questions on the clusters, there are three questions – numbers 38, 39 and 40 – which invite you to compare poems from different clusters, rather than poems within the same group. As long as you have studied more than one cluster, this represents a good additional choice. Questions 38 and 39 will ask you to select poems from two particular clusters, whereas Question 40 will allow you to choose from any of the poems in any cluster. There are some examples of cross-cluster questions at the end of the Poetry section.

To summarize, you should:
- read all your texts again in your revision period
- work out your own point of view on each text, and be able to support it with evidence
- choose texts which you can write about most effectively
- remember that the questions will ask you to compare, and be prepared for any combination
- remember that you must include at least one pre-twentieth-century poem in your poetry answer.

2 Sitting the examination

- First – don't forget to bring your texts with you!
- The next thing to do is to set about making good use of your time. The examination is two hours long - so obviously, as both answers you write will carry the same marks, you should aim to divide your time equally between the two. Within the time you have for each question, it is important *not* to start writing too quickly. The NEAB has built time for planning and thought into the timing of the exam – so use it!

- Making a good choice of question to tackle is vital. Give yourself the time to read your possible choices carefully, looking for the question you're happiest with in each section, either because it centres on the texts you want to write about, or because it asks an interesting question that you think you can write about well. When you've made your choice, read the question again *very carefully*, identifying exactly what the elements of the question are. After all, you've spent a lot of time reading the texts, so it's worth spending a little time on reading what you're asked to do with them!

- Next, plan your answer. With the poetry question, you'll need to choose the poems that will fit best into your answer, remembering that you must include at least one pre-twentieth-century poem. You may choose simply to follow the prompts in the question, though as long as you tackle them all it doesn't matter how you fit them in. You must try to construct a logical order to your response, which allows you to answer the question. The sections in this book called **Structuring a response** may help you here. Telling the story is *not* the way to answer! You should be thinking about what the writer had to say, and how he or she said it.

- Now you can start writing. Remember what you've learned about the pieces, and to support what you say with references to the texts, and you'll be fine! Remember, too, that every question will ask you to write about *how* the writers have written, as well as *what* they have said.

Prose

1

Superman and Paula Brown's New Snowsuit by Sylvia Plath

Sylvia Plath was born in 1932 in the USA. She married the English poet, Ted Hughes, in 1956 and settled in England, but separated in 1962; a year later she committed suicide. She wrote this autobiographical story while she was still at college.

Glossary

Dali Salvador Dali was a surrealist painter, whose most famous pictures showed collections of objects associated with dreamlike symbols in bold, colourful landscapes.

Icarus In Greek legend, Icarus was the son of Daedalus, an Athenian craftsman. To help them to escape from prison in Crete, Daedalus made wings so that he and his son could fly over the sea. But Icarus flew too close to the sun, and when the wax on his wings melted, he fell into the sea and drowned.

Read and revise

This story is quite complex. Read it right through once before tackling any of the questions.

1   Paragraph one mentions 'the changing colours of those days'.
   - Look at paragraphs two and three, and underline all the words that mention or suggest colours or light. Notice how many there are.
   - Now look at the last paragraph of the story. Underline all the words that mention or suggest colour. Which period of the *narrator's* life do the bright colours belong to?

2   Look at paragraphs two, three and four, down to 'the motors of a thousand planes'.
   - Underline all the words that suggest excitement, myths and fairy tales.
   - Now underline all the words that refer to dreams and flying.
   - You should now have a lot of words underlined in the first four paragraphs. If you look at them together, what do they tell you about the narrator's feelings about her childhood?

3 In paragraph three, the narrator remembers 'making up dreams'. What is she able to do with these dreams?

4 Look at lines 41–7. What unpleasant things are mentioned here? Make a note of them.

5 Now look at the short paragraph beginning 'The threat of war was seeping in everywhere.' (lines 67–70)
- Find references to both play and war here.
- Why do you think Sheldon 'became a Nazi'? (Look back at question 4.)

6 Look at the paragraph beginning 'The movie was about . . .'. (lines 90–3). In the second sentence, how does the writer emphasize that this was something very different from the imaginary world of childhood? Look at the shape of the sentence as well as the words that are used.

7 In the film the Japanese soldiers are shown torturing the prisoners, and killing them and laughing. Who else in the story have we already seen behaving like this?

8 When the narrator goes to bed after seeing the war film, and closes her eyes, she sees very different pictures in her mind from those she sees at the beginning of the story. How are they different? What can't she do now?

9 The second part of the story begins with 'Saturday was bitterly cold . . .' (line 106) It's about a children's game.
- Look at the first sentence beginning 'Saturday' and underline all the adjectives. What sort of mood is being created here?

10 Find the moment when Paula falls over, and look at the two sentences beginning 'No one said a word.'
- There's a reminder of the beginning of the story here. What is it?
- How does the author create a sense of something coming to an end in the second sentence? Underline all the words that help to suggest this. (Think about what a window blind does.)

11 When the other children look at the narrator, they have 'a strange joy' in their eyes.
- What does this remind you of, earlier in the story?
- What do you think the author is suggesting here about the nature of children?
- Do you think this can be extended to human nature in general?

12 Now read right down to 'Only tell me how it really happened' (line 180). Do you think Mother and Uncle Frank believe the girl? What details make you think they do, or don't?

13 Read the next paragraph where the narrator says she 'can't make it any different'. Why can't she? How is this different to what she used to be able to do?

14 Read to the end of the story. You've already noticed how the dominant colours in the last paragraph are different from the colours at the beginning.
  • Can you now say why they are different? What do the dark colours represent?
  • How are you reminded of the early paragraphs here?
  • 'Nothing held, nothing was left.' Of what?
  • '. . . and the real world, and the difference'. What do you think these words mean, and why do you think the author chooses to end with them?

Final thoughts

Read the whole story once more, thinking about the title. How do the two things, 'Superman' and 'Paula Brown's New Snowsuit', *symbolize* the 'difference' in the narrator's life that came about during this period?

Questions

Foundation Tier

How do **Superman and Paula Brown's New Snowsuit** and **The Genius** show some of the difficulties of growing up?

You should write about:
  • the difficulties the central characters have with other children
  • the difficulties the central characters have with adults
  • how they feel about the difficulties they face
  • how the authors of the stories show their difficulties.

Higher Tier

Several of the stories in the **Anthology** are about moments in people's lives when they realize something important. Write about **Superman and Paula Brown's New Snowsuit** and **one** other story of your choice, showing how the authors of the stories reveal these moments.

You should write about:
  • the realizations that the people in the story come to
  • the similarities and the differences in the experiences they have
  • how the authors use language to present their experiences
  • how the authors *structure* their stories.

The Test by Henry Slesar

Henry Slesar was born in 1927. He is an American writer of mystery, detective and science fiction stories.

Glossary

playing possum pretending to be dead before 'coming back to life'
peroration summing up a speech to the court
indomitable undefeatable
facetiousness making jokes at inappropriate times

Read and revise

Read the story through once, so that you are clear about the ending – if not about the truth!

1   Look at the first 22 lines of the story, as far as 'You don't need me'. Does Vernon want to take the case? Underline the words that indicate his attitude – what he feels, what he does, the way he says things.

2   Looking at the same lines, what reasons can you find for Mr Blesker's belief that his son is innocent? (Vernon sums it up in a phrase. Mark it if you can find it, and think about the end of the story.)

3   Now read as far as the first break in the story (after 'I'll think it over,' line 50). What reasons does Vernon have *not* to take the case? Why does he take it? Try to find and mark the exact phrases that show his reasons.

4   Read the next 16 lines, up to 'Don't think this is going to be easy' (lines 65–6).
    • Underline all the words that state or imply Benjy's age.
    • Underline all the words or phrases that state or imply Vernon's attitude to him.
    How do you think the author wants the reader to respond to Benjy at this point?

5   Now read the rest of Vernon's interrogation of Benjy, up to 'I got a father!' (line 137).
    • Again find the words in this section that state or imply Vernon's attitude to Benjy.
    • Does Vernon believe Benjy at this point? Mark the evidence.
    • Does the reader believe Benjy at this point? Why, or why not?

6 'I'm not your son! I got a father!' (line 137)
- What is the main difference between Vernon and Mr Blesker? Have a look at your responses so far.
- What similarity does Vernon see between father and son, when he meets the father again in the next paragraph?

7 Read the next section, from 'Like father, like son' to 'He seemed satisfied' (line 160).
- Exactly what does Mr Blesker suggest as Vernon's reason for wanting Benjy to plead guilty? Underline the sentence that tells you.
- Is he right? Find the word that tells you.

8 This story is called **The Test**. Vernon is tested here by Mr Blesker. What is Blesker 'satisfied' about?

9 Read the first section of the court case, up to 'he felt as forlorn as Benjy Blesker looked' (line 161–204). How do things go badly for Vernon and Benjy here? Do they make you think that Benjy is guilty, or not?

10 The next short section ('On the eve of the fourth day . . . I didn't do it!', lines 205–18) is between Vernon and Benjy. Do you think Vernon believes Benjy is guilty? How do you know?

11 Now move to the section beginning 'There was a weekend hiatus' (line 235) and read to 'admitting the truth' (line 240).
- Underline the word used twice in reference to the old man (apart from 'old').
- Decide what this word means – and look back at question 2.
- What effect might this attitude have on Benjy, in Vernon's opinion?

12 Read to the end of the conversation between Vernon and Hagerty (lines 304–5).
'You've saved my life, Doc.'
'*Your* life?' Hagerty said dryly.
- Why does Hagerty question Vernon's phrase?
- What does the word 'dryly' tell you about Hagerty's attitude to Vernon?
- What does he think Vernon's motives are? Is he right?

13 Read the next conversation between Vernon and Benjy (lines 308–32).
- Do you think Vernon believes Benjy at this point? How do you know? Mark the evidence.
- Do you believe Benjy at this point? Why?

14 Read lines 401–4, after the jury's verdict, carefully looking for evidence of the attitudes of all three characters.
- How does Benjy react here? Find the words that tell you his reaction.
- Do you think he's guilty or not, now? Why?

15 What is Vernon's attitude now?

16 The last 8 lines are about Mr Blesker. Does he care whether his son is guilty or not? Find any words which seem to suggest his attitude.
- The author chooses 'together' as the last word of the story. Why? (There's a clue in the rest of the sentence.)

Final thoughts

- Look at your responses to the questions again, or re-read the story. You will see how the author has constantly played with the reader's response to Benjy.
- The story follows Vernon's thoughts and feelings – what effect do you think this has?
- The ending is rather a surprise. How has the author prepared us for the ending? Think about what you have found out about the father. Like Vernon, you might find it frustrating not to know for sure whether Benjy is guilty or not. Leaving it open tells you something about the author's priorities, though. What is most important to him in the end?

Questions

Foundation Tier

Many authors deal with the complicated relationships between young people and their parents. Write about this aspect of **The Test** and **one other** story from the selection which deals with a parent/child relationship.

You should write about:
- what the parents feel about their children
- what the children feel about their parents
- what similarities and differences you can see in the relationships
- how the authors of the stories portray the relationships.

Higher Tier

The Test and **Your Shoes** both have unusual endings. Think about them.

You should write about:
- what you think is unusual in the endings
- how each author prepares the reader for the endings
- how language and *structure* are used to make the endings work
- what similarities and differences you can see, and which ending you prefer.

Kiss Miss Carol by Farrukh Dhondy

Farrukh Dhondy was born in India in 1944. He taught English in comprehensive schools in London before becoming a full-time writer in 1982.

Glossary

A Christmas Carol is a famous novel by Charles Dickens. Scrooge, a wealthy but mean businessman, dislikes Christmas, but after seeing frightening visions of Christmas Past, Present and Future on Christmas Eve, including a vision of what his own death will be like if he does not mend his ways, he wakes on Christmas morning a changed man. He sends a turkey to his clerk Bob Cratchit and his family, which includes the crippled Tiny Tim.

Read and revise

1   Neither the white community nor the Bengali community is presented in a straightforward way in this story. The most obvious hostility comes from the people in the van at the end.
    • How exactly do they insult the Bengalis?
    • Underline what you think is the worst thing they say.
    • What is the most threatening thing they do?

2   Look at the description of 'the white people hurrying towards the train station' early in the story (line 68). How do they feel about the Bengalis? Are they kind and understanding? Mark the words and phrases that sum up their attitude.

3   For Jolil, the most important white person is his teacher, Miss Ingram. Skim through the story to find out how the author presents Miss Ingram. Look for what she says to Jolil, and to others, and for words that describe how she looks and behaves. 'She smiled and said . . .' is one example, but there are a lot more.

4   Is the school presented favourably or unfavourably by the author? Apart from Miss Ingram, think about:
    • the headmaster
    • Jolil's classmates
    • what the school represents for Jolil and his father at the end.
    • how the play is received.

5 Jolil's father is the most important Bengali character in the story, apart from Jolil himself. What is his attitude to white people? Think about:
- what Jolil thinks his father's attitude to Miss Ingram will be – and why he thinks this
- the way he refers to the men in the van.

6 What details does the author use to show that Jolil's father is loyal to Bengali culture? Find and underline:
- a detail from paragraph one which suggests this
- the way he dresses
- his attitude to the play
- his attitude to his home village.

7 Jolil's attitude to his father is not as simple as it seems. What is his attitude towards him in paragraph one, and how does he feel about the possibility of his father coming to see the play (lines 49–58)? Underline the phrase in the next paragraph (lines 59–61) that tells you that his attitude isn't quite what it appears to be.

8 Jolil wants to say to Miss Ingram, 'My Dad is Scrooge'.
- Is this fair? Why might he think his father is like Scrooge?
- What are his father's real motives? Look at the description of him after he has explained to Jolil about the extra work (lines 147–8).

9 What is the difference between Jolil's father's attitude to the village in Bangladesh, and that of Khalil and Jolil? Where does Jolil seem to belong?

10 Although Jolil is happy in school, he does notice some differences between himself and the white children. Find and underline the sentences which tell you this.

11 Jolil thinks of lots of lies that he could tell during this story, although actually he doesn't lie very often. Find some of his imaginary lies, and decide why he wants to tell them instead of the truth.

12 When Jolil and his father set out with the finished linings, Jolil is told to learn two things (lines 220–1). What are they? In what way are these instructions *ironic*? (Think about what Jolil should be doing.)

13 When Miss Ingram sees Jolil, she says, 'I thought you'd been kidnapped or something.' (lines 280–1) How does this link up with something Jolil mentions earlier in the story?

14 The ending is a happy one, apparently – Jolil and his father have escaped from their attackers, and Jolil performs his part in the play. But is everything really all right in the end?

Final thoughts

Look over the story again. Why do you think it is called **Kiss Miss Carol**? You might think about:

- why the story is set at Christmas
- why the author chooses **A Christmas Carol** as the school play
- Miss Ingram.

Questions

Foundation Tier

Jolil's relationship with his father is difficult. Write about **Kiss Miss Carol** and **one other** story of your choice where there are problems between children and older family members.

You should write about:

- the reasons for the problems
- how the children and adults feel about each other
- any similarities and differences you can see between the stories
- how the authors present the problems.

Higher Tier

Jolil in **Kiss Miss Carol** and the grandfather in **Flight** both have really difficult decisions to make. Compare the two stories, showing how the authors present their characters' feelings and decisions.

You should write about:

- the nature of the decisions
- how the two characters try to deal with their situations
- how the authors help you to understand their decisions by the way in which they write.

Flight by Doris Lessing

Doris Lessing was born in 1919. She lived in Africa from 1924 until 1949, when she moved to England, with the manuscript of her first novel which became a best-seller. She has won a number of literary prizes, including the W. H. Smith Award in 1986.

Glossary

frangipani a tropical tree with scented white flowers

Read and revise

Read the story right through once, focusing on the old man's emotions.

1 The author (and perhaps the old man) clearly connect the granddaughter with the favourite pigeon. Look at paragraph one and underline the words that describe this bird. Think how they might apply to the girl as well.

2 Find and underline the one word in paragraph two which sums up the old man's mood. Now look at paragraph five, beginning 'His mood shifted.'
   - Underline the words in this paragraph which identify his mood now, and notice the change from paragraph two.
   - What has caused the change in mood?
   - With your knowledge of the whole story, what does the action of shutting the bird into its box represent? Look at what the old man does, and what he says. Look up *symbol* in the **Glossary** (page 110).

3 Read the short paragraph beginning 'Hey!' (line 26). Which words tell you about the girl's attitude to her grandfather at this point?

4 Look at the brief conversation between them, beginning 'Waiting for Steven' (line 29). Look for the attitudes and feelings here. What does the phrase 'curling like claws' remind you of?

5 Look at the two sentences beginning 'Misery went to his head' (lines 39–41). Underline the single words about the old man and the girl which contrast directly with each other.

6 Look at the paragraph which begins 'Growling' (line 46). What reasons can you see here for the old man feeling and behaving in the way he does? Underline the words which tell you this.

7 Read the conversation between the old man and his daughter (lines 73–92). What is his daughter's attitude to him? Look at what she says to him, the way she's described, and how she speaks. Which of the two seems the older here?

8 The grandfather says to his daughter, 'Can't we keep her a bit longer?'
- What does this tell you about the relationship between them?
- Who has the greater authority in the household?

9 Look at the paragraph beginning 'Do you like it?' (line 112)
- How are the girl and Steven behaving towards the old man? Underline the words that describe their feelings, their attitude, their intentions.
- Why are their eyes described as 'lying', do you think? What have they suggested that might not be true?
- Who do you think is describing their eyes as 'lying'? The grandfather? The author? Or the young people themselves?
- Is the girl's affection a lie? Think about the last sentence of the story.

10 The girl advises her grandfather that he should 'shut up' the new bird 'until it knows this is its home'. Why is it *ironic* that she should say this? Look at your responses to questions 2 and 5. Think again about the girl's reaction at the end of the story.

11 Look at the phrase 'Released by his half-deliberate anger' (line 123). Steven and the girl now feel free to move away from him.
- Why has the author chosen the word 'released' here, and why has she placed it at the beginning of the sentence and the paragraph?

12 In the paragraph beginning 'Released', how does the old man see the young couple now? How does their behaviour make him feel?

13 'They had forgotten him again. Well, so they should' (lines 127–8). In terms of the development of the old man's emotions, how is this an important moment?

14 The paragraph ends 'and took out his favourite'. The author does not say 'his favourite *pigeon*'. Why not? What is she indicating here?

15 ' "*Now* you can go," he said aloud. He held it poised, ready for flight, while he looked down the garden towards the boy and the girl. Then, clenched in the pain of loss . . .'
- Why '*Now*'? Think about your response to question 13.
- The old man clearly knows what releasing the bird will represent. Think about where he looks before he releases it, and think why releasing a homing pigeon (which he knows will return) causes him to feel 'the pain of loss'.

16 '. . . the whole afternoon had stilled to watch his gesture of self-command' (lines 138–9).
- What has the old man made himself do?
- Find the single word in the next short paragraph which conveys his mood as he looks up to the sky. How is this a change from earlier in the story? Why has his mood changed, do you think?

17 Look at the description of the birds flying, from 'The cloud of shining silver birds' to 'the shelter of night' (lines 142–8).
- Mark all the words here which refer to or suggest light and shade – and make a distinction between them.
- Which type of word (light or shade) has the author used to refer to the sky, and which to the ground?
- Which type of word has the author used to refer to release, and which to coming home?

18 Look at the description of the girl in the last paragraph.
- Referring to your response to the previous question, how does the author continue the light/shade idea here, and what does she suggest through it?
- Why do you think the girl is in tears as she looks at her grandfather? What do you think she may have realized as she watched the birds?

Final thoughts

Read the story right through again, this time looking at the girl's emotions and how they change. Compare the development of her feelings to the changes in her grandfather's emotions. Why has the situation reversed?

Consider how *you* feel about the grandfather at the end of the story, and how you felt about him at the beginning. How has Doris Lessing made you change your view, and your expectations?

Questions

Foundation Tier

Flight and **Your Shoes** both show an older person wanting to restrict a younger member of the family. Consider both stories.

You should write about:
- the older people's reasons for wanting to restrict the younger people
- how the young people respond to their situations
- how the authors show the feelings of both the older and younger people
- who you sympathize with, and why.

Higher Tier

In **Flight** Doris Lessing uses pigeons as a symbol of something else. Write about how she does this, and how the writer of another story from the **Anthology** uses the same technique.

You should write about:
- the symbols and what they represent
- why the authors have chosen these particular symbols
- how the authors show that these things are symbols
- what the authors gain from using the symbols.

Your Shoes by Michèle Roberts

Michèle Roberts is half-English and half-French. She was poetry editor of the feminist magazine Spare Rib *from 1975 to 1977.*

Read and revise

There's a lot to look for in this story. It's written as a first-person narrative which begins as a letter from a mother to her runaway daughter – though you may wonder if it's still a letter by the end. Read the story right through before looking at any of the questions.

1   The woman reveals a lot about herself and her past.
   - Look first at the paragraph beginning 'Your father didn't mean it' (line 59). Which words are used here to describe the woman's family, and her father? Underline them.
   - Look through the rest of the story for instances of what she had to do when she was a child, and what she couldn't do.

2   The woman's relationship with her mother was clearly very difficult, and affected her considerably.
   - Look for some of the criticisms she has of her mother, and notice how the author suggests them.
   - 'There was so much I wanted to say to her and now it's too late' (lines 103–4). Why didn't she say these things to her? What is she doing now, in effect?

3   The woman's relationship with her father might seem easier than that with her mother. Find some examples of her preference for her father. But it's not as simple as that. Read from the paragraph beginning 'I had a white wedding' (line 147) to line 166.
   - What would her father have done to her if he'd known the truth about her?
   - What didn't he do for her when she was a baby, and why?

4   Her own marriage is not quite what it seems.
   - What feelings did she *not* experience at her wedding? Find the sentences that describe it.
   - Look for the sentence in paragraph five of the story that describes how a 'husband and wife' should behave. What does this reveal about the woman's relationship with her husband?

- Now look at the paragraph beginning 'I don't think you have a clue how we feel' (line 83). What don't this couple do? Think about the way the woman describes her own childhood and what the connection might be.
- 'After all this is his house' (line 101). What does this comment reveal about the woman?

5 The mother has a number of conflicting emotions about her child. Look for examples of:
- her criticism of her daughter's behaviour
- her lack of understanding of her daughter
- her jealousy of her daughter.

6 Look at the paragraph beginning 'Of course I wanted you' (line 155).
- How does the mother see herself here?
- What did she not do for her child? (Think about what she's doing now.)
- How did she try to be a good mother? Find some examples.

7 Look at the last 8 lines of the story (lines 193–200). What emotion does the woman feel most strongly now? What does she want to do for her daughter? Do you think she's ever revealed this before?

8 The author shows us the woman through a first-person narrative, so that we follow her train of thoughts and feelings.
- Sometimes feelings are stated directly, such as 'I might go mad'. Find another example of a direct statement of emotion in the story.
- In other instances we have to decide whether the first-person narrative is reliable. In the paragraph beginning 'Your father didn't mean it' (line 59), she writes, 'We've given you everything a child could possibly want'. Is this true? Do you think she believes it?

9 The woman in the story is in a state of extreme grief. 'If I wrap my arms around myself and hold tight it keeps the pain in . . . If I keep my mouth pursed tight I can't scream or throw up' (lines 21–3).
- What does she want to do with her pain? Think about her life when she was younger and living at home, and then her married life.
- What does she do during the story, actually?

10 The author uses shoes in all sorts of ways in the story, including in the title. Look up the definition of *symbol* in the **Glossary** (page 110).
- At the end of the story the woman behaves in a very unusual way with the shoes, but the reader has been prepared for this. 'Someone . . . might pick up a shoe from the rug and hold it like a baby' (lines 6–7). 'I locked the wardrobe door on those rebellious shoes' (line 12). Who is being identified with the shoes here?

- 'They're best in here with me, I think, safe and warm in bed. Tucked up tight' (lines 180–1). Who are the shoes representing (or symbolizing), and at what age?

11 Perhaps the shoes don't just represent one person. What is it that the woman, her mother and her daughter all have in common? Find the reference and underline it. Think about the exact physical position the woman ends up in. She's curled up, enclosed, and sucks the laces of the new shoes. What does this resemble? What are the shoes a symbol of now?

Final thoughts

This is a complicated, sophisticated story. Take a break from it and then read it again, thinking about these two issues:

- 'It didn't do me any harm' (line 65). What harm was done to the woman in her childhood?
- There are a number of possible interpretations of the ending. Is it a positive ending, or a negative one? Is the woman sliding into madness, or coming to terms with something? It might help to look closely at what she says, thinks and feels here – in ways that perhaps she has never done before.

Questions

Foundation Tier

The mother in **Your Shoes** and the grandfather in **Flight** both become very distressed about certain events that take place. Write about how the distress of **both** characters is shown.

You should write about:
- the causes of their distress
- how they deal with it
- the similarities and differences in their situations
- how the authors use language and structure to explain their situations.

Higher Tier

Several of the stories in this section deal with strong emotions. Write about **Your Shoes** and **one other** story from the **Anthology** which does so.

You should write about:
- the emotions that are shown in the stories you have chosen
- how the authors convey these emotions to the reader.

The Darkness
Out There by Penelope Lively

> *Penelope Lively was born in 1933. She has written a number of novels for adults and*
> *children, and she often writes about how the past affects the present, as she does here.*

Read and revise

Read the story once without writing anything down. Then read it again, noticing how the two people Sandra meets seem different to her at the end. Why does this happen, and where does it begin? Working through the suggestions below will help you to answer these questions.

1 Sandra likes things to be pleasant and 'nice'. Find and mark as many places as you can where this is shown or suggested. It might be in what she says or does; look at the words the author uses to convey her thoughts, too.

2 At the beginning of the story Sandra is still rather childish, but at the end she has had to grow up. Where do you think this process starts? Mark all the possible places in the last three pages.

3 What is Sandra made to think differently about at the end of the story? There are a number of things, and people too. Identify them, looking closely at the last page. Look back at the early descriptions in the story of old people, the wood, and Kerry, and think how things have changed.

4 'Everything is not as it appears to be, oh no' (line 384).
   Look at the description of Mrs Rutter in lines 97–9. Which words do not seem to fit in with the rest of the description? Mark them. Find the references to her eyes in lines 110–17, as well. How does this prepare us for what is revealed about Mrs Rutter later?

5 Mrs Rutter says, 'I've got a sympathy with young people' twice. Think of the ways this seems to be true, and the ways it isn't. Find examples in the text.

6 Penelope Lively seems concerned with the way children see things differently as they grow older. Look at pages 56–7 again very carefully, and find places where she suggests these things, sometimes with unexpected details, or in the language she uses.

7 Most of the story is written from Sandra's point of view, though without using 'I'.
   • Look at lines 1–15 to see how this is done. What are you told about what she does/sees/thinks/feels?
   • Who does the story focus on in lines 256–349? Why, do you think?
   • From lines 350–84, the author gives Sandra's point of view again. Why?

8 Sandra thinks, 'it's different for boys' (line 180).
   • Find the moments in the story when males or females seem to act or think as they might be 'expected' to. How does this change in the last few pages?
   • Think about what Mrs Rutter says, and the way Kerry behaves. How does the author show these changes? Mark some words or phrases.

9 Read from 'Mrs Rutter picked out a tea-leaf with the tip of the spoon' (line 284) to 'Tit for tat, I said to Dot' (line 325). Notice how many times Mrs Rutter interrupts Sandra and Kerry when they start to speak. What is the author showing about Mrs Rutter here, do you think?

10 The author uses light and darkness a lot in this story.
   • Go back to the beginning of the story, and skim through the first part, when Sandra is walking by the wood, until she gets to Mrs Rutter's house. Underline the references to light (including sunshine) and dark. What does Sandra think about light and dark? What sort of things does she connect with them?
   • Now look at the last page, and the descriptions of the wood here. How has Sandra's view of 'darkness' changed from the beginning? What does 'darkness' seem to represent now?

11 Sandra comes to an alarming realization on the last page. What is it, and why is it alarming?

Final thoughts

Read the story once more, noticing all the things you've marked. At the end, what do you think 'the darkness out there' really is?

This story is about many things. What do you think the main themes are?

Think about:
• the difficulties of growing up
• how surface appearances can be false
• male and female behaviour – and how your expectations can be wrong.

Questions

Foundation Tier

Sandra in **The Darkness Out There** and the narrator in **Superman and Paula Brown's New Snowsuit** both have to face very unpleasant situations. Write about how the authors of the stories show these situations.

You should write about:
- what their situations are
- how they feel about what happens to them
- the similarities and differences you can see in their situations
- how the authors use language and shape their stories so as to present their situations to the reader.

Higher Tier

Sandra sees things differently by the end of **The Darkness Out There**. Write about this and **one other** story from the **Anthology** where somebody's outlook changes in a similar way, showing how the authors present their characters' experiences.

You should write about:
- the changes that take place
- how and why the changes come about
- the way the authors use language and *structure* to show change
- any similarities or differences you can see in the experiences or the way they are presented.

The Genius by Frank O'Connor

Frank O'Connor was the pen name of Michael O'Donovan, who lived in Ireland from 1903 to 1966. This story was first published in a collection in 1953.

Glossary

Temperance abstinence from alcoholic drink, but it can also mean moderation or self-restraint.

Read and revise

Read the story right through once, concentrating on the boy's character and his relationship with his parents.

1   In a first-person narrative like this, the author has to convey the character of the speaker mainly through the character's own words. Read the first five paragraphs again, as far as 'I intended to supply the deficiency' (line 48).
    - What evidence is there of the boy's cleverness in paragraph two?
    - Look at the sentence about kicking a ball in paragraph three. Which word conveys how the boy kicks the ball, and also something about him? Underline it.
    - Look at the sentence about little girls, in the same paragraph. What does the boy want from people? What is unusual in the phrase that describes what he wants (remember how old he is)?
    - Look at his account of an exploration from his house (lines 33–7). How is the exploration typical of a child? Again, what does he want (there's a word repeated from paragraph three)?

2   The boy's relationship with his father is difficult.
    - Look for and underline words and phrases that convey the father's attitude and feelings towards the boy.
    - His father's friends have 'normal, bloodthirsty, illiterate children' (lines 60–1). How would the father like the boy to behave? What is funny about the words 'normal, bloodthirsty, illiterate children'?
    - Look at the first conversation in the story between the boy and his father (lines 68–75), and underline the words that tell you how the boy behaves towards his father.

3 The boy is much closer to his mother. Re-read the first half of the story, up to the point where he meets Una, and underline the sentences which tell you about the mother's attitude to the boy.

4 Look at the paragraph beginning 'But whatever the world wanted to rob me of' (line 126).
- What does the boy want again here?
- What sort of attitude can you see behind his father's joke?

5 At the end of the story the boy's mother says, 'You reminded her of her little brother that was killed, of course – that was why' (lines 346–7). Now look back at lines 171–82. Which two sentences does the author put next to each other to make the truth of the mother's statement clear to the reader? Notice Una's mother's reaction, too, in the same paragraph.

6 Look at the paragraph beginning 'I replied politely that I did' (line 193).
- How does the author remind us that the *narrator* is an older man looking back to childhood? Mark where he does this.

7 The author also tells us about the narrator's character through other people's reactions. Why do you think his discussions are 'immediately interrupted' at the Dwyers' house, but not at home? There may be several reasons for this.

8 Look at the narrator's reaction when he is told that they are on the spot where little John Joe was killed. What does it tell you about him? (Again, remember his age.) Although this is tragic, it is also very funny. What is humorous, exactly? Look at the words the author chooses.

9 What is *ironic* about the boy's statement that he 'had never been convinced' by his mother's explanation about babies compared with the other explanations, and his conclusion that her theory was 'now definitely out of fashion'?

10 Towards the end of the story the boy becomes more aware of his feelings.
- Find the sentence about two pages from the end where he uses the phrase 'for the first time', and underline the sentence. Why does he feel this way?
- How does the boy feel about his mother when Una comes to tea? Underline the words which tell you. Why does he feel this way?

11 'I saw that love was a game that two people couldn't play at without pushing, just like football' (lines 136–8).

- How has the boy reached this conclusion?
- Why is it humorous?
- What does it show about the boy? Consider all the emotions he experiences from the moment that Una comes out of the gates at the end of the story – how has he changed from the beginning?

Final thoughts

Read the story again, looking out for the way the author makes the narrator both unusual and a typical small boy. What do you think the main ideas in this story are? Think about:

- growing up
- parent/child relationships
- the differences between men and women.

Questions

Foundation Tier

The boy in **The Genius** and Jolil in **Kiss Miss Carol** are both children who don't completely understand the world around them. Write about both stories.

You should write about:

- what they don't understand, and why
- whether you think they reach a better understanding during the course of the stories
- how the authors of the stories show what happens to the characters, and how they think
- any similarities and differences you can see in the characters' situations.

Higher Tier

The Genius shows a child's view of the world. Write about how Frank O'Connor and the author of **one other** story in the **Anthology** convey the child's point of view.

You should write about:

- how the children see adults in the stories
- how the children see the world around them
- how the authors' use of language and *structure* conveys the children's points of view
- any similarities or differences you can see in the children, and how they are presented.

The examination questions on the stories in the **Anthology** will ask you to write about two stories, and to compare them. When you're thinking about the individual stories in the selection, and especially when you're revising them before the exams, it's a good idea to think about them together. Some of the stories are quite similar to each other, either in what they're about or in the way that they're written, but at the same time some are very different. Even those that are alike in *subject* might be very different in *style*, and you might be asked about this too.

In this section we're going to look at two stories which could easily be compared, though you might be asked about any combination. The suggestions are presented in note form – the sort of notes you might make in preparing for your answer. You'll need to add plenty of evidence from the text for a full answer.

Two stories which could be looked at together and compared are **Flight** by Doris Lessing and **Your Shoes** by Michèle Roberts. One way to look at them together is to think about the *content*, such as the feelings, attitudes and ideas in the stories, and then at the *style* – how the writers have expressed their ideas. The exam questions often ask you to explore the stories in this way, too, though you certainly don't have to be rigid in following this approach. Here are some of the things that might occur to you when looking at these two stories.

Content

- *Situations* similar – older person wants to restrain younger. Grandfather/grandchild in *Flight*, mother/daughter in *Your Shoes*. Young people ready to leave.

- Older people's *feelings and attitudes* similar – both hurt, both selfish. Both resent the actions of the young.

- Stories are different too, e.g. the endings, though both result from older person's attitude. Grandfather accepts, forces himself to change; mother will not change, locked into grief. Young people respond differently. Granddaughter in **Flight** calms her grandfather and loves him, as shown by distress at end; daughter in your **Your Shoes** apparently does not, though not shown.

Style

- *Tone* emotional in both – shown differently. **Flight** uses third person – we see old man objectively, and from daughter's and granddaughter's point of view. **Your Shoes** uses first person, and letter form. Emotions and events through mother's eyes only – have to infer things about central figure which are given directly in **Flight**. Present tense – unfolds dramatically.

- *Symbolism* used in both stories and titles. Pigeon in **Flight** = granddaughter. The old man wants 'his favourite' to stay, but at the end deliberately releases her. Mother wants to restrain daughter – shoes represent her: 'I locked the wardrobe door on those rebellious shoes'. At the end 'safe and warm' with the mother, in her mind. Dramatic climax in both stories depends on central symbol.

When you set about responding to a question in the examination, it's important to take some time to plan your work. In this section there's an example of a plan for a particular question – but remember that there could be a number of other ways to plan a successful answer.

As well as questions which name particular stories, there will also be one question which allows you to choose any two stories you like. Suppose, for example, that the question in the exam was:

Compare two stories where characters face difficult situations.

You should write about:
- **what the difficulties are**
- **how the characters deal with the difficulties**
- **what you think the authors want to say, and how they say it**
- **how you respond to the situations, and how you think the authors make you respond in this way.**

You could choose almost any of the stories to answer this question. If, for example, you decided to use the same two stories as we've looked at in **Comparing Stories** – **Flight** and **Your Shoes** – how would you go about it? Bullet points have been provided to help you to think along the right lines. One way of structuring a response is simply to follow the bullets one by one, if these are offered – but you don't *have* to do it this way. You *do* have to cover what they suggest at some point in your writing, though, so it's important to look carefully at what they're asking.

Looking at the bullet points in this question, it's clear that the first two are asking something about *content*, and the second two about *style*. The two are obviously very closely related, and you might not want to divide them in this way, but let's suppose that your structure simply followed the bullets. The plan, with a little detail to indicate what you're going to write about in each section, might look something like this:

- **what the difficulties are**
  Flight: outlines the grandfather's reluctance to let the girl go/ the girl's problems dealing with her grandfather, and her distress when he lets her go.

  Your Shoes: the mother's problems coming to terms with her daughter's flight/ the daughter's reasons for leaving – possibly.

- **how the characters deal with the difficulties**

  Flight: grandfather's anger/spite, appeal to daughter, overcoming by recognizing inevitability, the release; girl's manipulation of the old man, but distress when she realizes the significance of his action.

  Your Shoes: mother's self-justification/criticism of daughter/madness.

- **what you think the authors want to say, and how they say it**

  Both about problems of letting young people grow up and leave home.

  Flight: story in third person lets us see grandfather's motives clearly – use of pigeon as symbol for girl and her release – flight in title.

  Your Shoes: first-person narrative to convey mother's feelings and her increasing madness as story unfolds – change on last page and attitude to shoes – shoes as symbol and in title.

- **how you respond to the situations, and how you think the authors make you respond in this way**

  Flight: perhaps eventual sympathy for the grandfather, and realizing that the girl is not heartless – after his 'gesture of self-command', the girl's distress and the author's use of light/shade/symbolism at the end.

  Your Shoes: perhaps horror at the woman's condition at the end? – created by the lapse into clear madness on the last page, the disjointed nature of the last few sentences, the use of symbolism at the end.

This is a pretty detailed plan, but when you go into the exam you should know the stories so well that you could write a plan like this without having to open your **Anthology** at all. You should probably only have to refer to it to look at some details. You might well think of a lot more to say as you write, which is fine, but if you stick to the outlines of your plan it will help you to answer the question effectively. *Remember* – you must give evidence from the texts to back up the points and comments that you make. Notice that in the plan the words 'perhaps' and 'possibly' are used. There are all kinds of things you *could* write, and when the question asks 'how you respond' it means just that – your own, individual, response. In the end, the examiner wants to know what *you* think.

Poetry

The Beggar Woman by William King

Read and revise

Read the poem through carefully to get the outline of the story, and then the details, clear in your mind. This is a *narrative* poem, one that tells a story, and has a very clear moral or message at the end. You need to understand how the poet builds up to, and emphasizes, the message.

1 The man is introduced in line 1 as 'A gentleman'. The seventeenth-century reader wouldn't have interpreted this as we might, in the sense of someone with good manners, but as a member of the wealthy upper-middle class. How does this affect your response to his attitude and behaviour towards the beggar woman, who we know is poor?

2 The man and his friends are hunting the hare. What does the man's description of the woman as 'other game' tell you about his attitude towards her?

3 Look at the description of the woman in lines 5 and 6, and underline the words which make us think favourably of her.

4 Lines 10–12 offer a picture of the two people going into the wood. How do their positions in relation to each other strengthen our view about the man's attitude to the woman? How does the poet make the woman appealing and the man unappealing in these lines?

5 In lines 15–34, the woman manoeuvres the man into a position from which she can safely escape. Work out the different stages of her plan, and jot them down with numbers in the right-hand margin of your **Anthology**. You should find four stages.

6 The woman refuses to simply put the child down, saying that it will cry. How does she cleverly present this to the man as a bad idea ?

7 The conversation in lines 15–34 seems to unwind in a leisurely way. At line 35, though, the pace changes.
   • How is the change emphasized? Look at the shape of the sentence.
   • Lines 35–40 are full of motion and force. Underline the words that the poet has chosen to create this feeling, and note your reasons for choosing them in the margin.

8 Before she leaves, the woman's 'message' to the man is about the consequences of his selfish actions, and taking responsibility for what he's done.

- Which phrase in the last two lines suggests what might have happened if the man had done what he intended to do?
- Which phrase suggests that the outcome for her would have lasted more than just the length of their time in the wood?

9 At the end of the poem, how has the man been given a taste of his own medicine? Is all your sympathy with the woman at the end?

Final thoughts

Read the poem again, and note how the poet has shaped your response to the two characters, and what happens between them.

Our Love Now by Martyn Lowery

Read and revise

1 It's clear that this relationship has had difficulties.

- What does the speaker, 'I', in the first column, liken the problem to in the second line?
- Look across to the first line of the reply by 'She' (line 27). Which word tells you that this is a reply?

2 The first speaker is obviously pacifying the second, trying to say that everything will be all right.

- Pick out the words that show this directly in stanza one, and underline them.
- Now look at the reply to this in stanza five. 'She' uses the same idea. Underline the words here that are linked to 'wound'.

3 Read all the stanzas on the left.

- Pick out the words in each stanza that are related to the idea in the opening line – 'wound', 'scald', and so on.

4 Now read the stanzas on the right.

- Pick out the words and phrases that contradict the ideas on the left. They're usually to do with change – for instance, in stanza two 'I' says that the scab 'will disappear', but 'She' says that the skin 'remains' bleached.

5 There's another pattern in the words, built around 'such is'.
- Pick out all these phrases throughout the poem from both columns.
- What do you think 'I' is trying to say by the repetition, 'Such is our love, such is our love'?
- In the answering voice, 'Such is our love now' takes on the opposite meaning. Look at the lines immediately before the last line in each stanza on the right-hand side. Pick out the words in each of them which insist on the damage done, and underline them.

6 The tone of the poem is very final at the end. The poet has made several choices of language, form and *structure* to make this happen.
- Each of the right-hand stanzas ends in 'now', except the last one. What effect does this have? Why isn't 'now' appropriate here?
- Who has the last word? What difference does that make?
- Imagine if the verses of the poem were the other way around, so that you read the right-hand column first and then the left. It would end, 'The breach in us can be mended'. What difference would that make?

Final thoughts

Read the poem right through again, noticing how all the 'She said' verses gradually depress the tone.

To His Coy Mistress by Andrew Marvell

Andrew Marvell (1621–78) was a diplomat and politician as well as a poet. He was MP for Hull from 1659. His lyric poetry, of which this is perhaps the best-known example, was virtually unknown until the twentieth century.

Glossary

coy shy, reluctant
Ganges a river in India
Humber a river in Yorkshire
languish droop
marble vault tomb
quaint odd, unusual
transpires ... fires gives off, breathes passion at every pore
slow-chapped slowly moving jaws
hue colour

Read and revise

This poem is a carefully structured formal argument designed to persuade the poet's mistress to go to bed with him without further delay. It is divided into three sections. If you look at the beginning of each section and find these words:

- 'Had we . . .' (i.e. 'If we had . . .')
- 'But . . .'
- 'Now, therefore . . .'

you can see the progress – the 'shape' – of the argument.

1   Look at the first section of the poem, up to line 20.
    - Underline all the references to places in this section, noticing the geographical range. The Humber is the river on which Hull stands.
    - Underline all the references to time, either direct or implied. Note that all the references are to increasingly lengthy periods of time.

2   Find all the references to love in this section. What is the poet emphasizing, and why is it important at the beginning of his argument?

3   Read the next stage in the argument (lines 21–32).
    - Which word in line 21 tells the reader (and the mistress) that everything the poet has said up to now is not factually true?
    - What do you notice about the rhythm and the length of the words? What is the effect of this?

4   Line 22 tells us that Time moves very quickly.
    - Underline the words that suggest speed.
    - Think about the image of Time's chariot. What do you normally associate with chariots?

5   In line 24, 'Deserts' implies a large, empty, endless, barren place. Why do you think the speaker uses this word?

6   In the first part of the argument, the poet praises the woman's physical features one by one.
    - What will happen to her beauty? Where will her body go?
    - Why do you think he mentions what worms will do to her?

7   What do 'dust' and 'ashes' in lines 29 and 30 remind you of?

8   Look at the final stage of the argument (lines 33–46).
    - Underline all the words and phrases that suggest urgency, beginning with 'Now'.
    - Underline all the words that suggest swift, even violent action – start with the verbs.

9 At the beginning of this last stage, the speaker focuses on the physical characteristics of his mistress.
   - What is the effect of 'while' in line 33?
   - Why do you think he compares her skin to 'morning dew'? Think about the time of day, and what happens to dew as the day moves on.

10 Line 40 is the one slow line in this section. Why do you think the poet slows down here? Think about what this line is referring to.

11 The lovers have to tear their pleasures 'Thorough the iron gates of life'. What does the poet mean by this? (Looking back to line 29 might help.)

12 Look at the last two lines. What do they suggest?
   - What word emphasizes that this is the conclusion to the argument?
   - Notice the length of the words in the last line and the word the whole poem ends on. Why do you think the poet ends this way?

Final thoughts

This is a wonderful and complex poem. Look back at your responses to the questions before reading through the poem again. Try reading it aloud this time, and make the last stage sound really urgent and passionate – the words will help you!

Rapunzstiltskin by Liz Lochhead

Liz Lochhead was born in Scotland in 1947 and worked as an art teacher before becoming a full-time writer in 1978. Her work is direct and witty and responds well to public performance.

Glossary

chignon a large, smooth knot of hair
cubit a unit of measurement

Read and revise

The poem is based on two traditional fairy tales, **Rapunzel** and **Rumpelstiltskin**. Before you read the poem, find out what happens in each story.

1 Liz Lochhead makes us feel as though we know a lot of the story already. How does she do this? Look at the first line.

2   Which word in the first line belongs to the language of old tales, particularly fairy tales? Underline it. Look for other similar words and phrases in the poem.

3   Men and women behave differently in this version of the fairy stories. Who has the right answer in **Rumpelstiltskin**? Who *hasn't* got the right answer here? Mark the first time that this is mentioned in the poem.

4   What is the Prince's main attraction, apart from the possibility of escape that he offers? Is this quality important, in the end?

5   The poet is careful to make her new version of the tales sound modern, by the words she uses as well as in the events that take place. Look at lines 11–18, and underline some of the words and phrases that are really modern.

6   Look at lines 22–7, and at the man's behaviour here. Think about:
    • the way he comes in
    • what he brings
    • what the girl is expected to do.
    How could his behaviour be described as typically male? What does this tell you about the poet's purpose in writing the poem?

7   Look at the Prince's answers. What does he think the girl wants him to say? What does she actually want from him?

8   The ending of the story is almost the same as the end of **Rumpelstiltskin** – but not quite. What is the most important difference?

Final thoughts

• How has the man failed to live up to the role of handsome Prince?
• Look back to the beginning of the poem. Has the girl's position improved at all? Look at her feelings at the beginning, before the Prince turns up.
• How do you respond to this poem? What do you think Liz Lochhead was trying to say? Does she succeed, by using the fairy-tale format? Do you find the poem funny, or not?

i wanna be yours by John Cooper Clarke

Read and revise

1   The mood of the poem is partly created by the use of repeated phrases. Underline these words and phrases, showing where they repeat.

2 *Rhyme* is a form of repetition, too, of sounds that link things together.
- Pick out all the rhymes. You'll soon see a pattern in the first two stanzas – the last line of each stanza is also part of the structure of the whole poem in the way that it links the stanzas together.
- Stanza three starts in the same way. Mark where it changes. What effect does this have? How does the poet bring the poem back to the original pattern at the end?
- Rhyme usually joins things so that they 'belong' together in some way – think about 'praise/gaze' in **To His Coy Mistress**, for example. This poet has fun linking things that don't go together at all. Pick out some examples.

3 This is a love poem and it's the unusual ideas the poet introduces – like being a vacuum cleaner – that make it so funny. Pick out some more unlikely comparisons and explain them.

4 Read the final stanza of the poem.
- According to the pattern of the rest of the poem, line 23 should move on to something different – but it doesn't, it continues the same thought. 'With deep devotion' is linked up with the line before and the line after. Which word in the line is used to link forward? How is the rhyme used to link forwards and backwards?
- 'Deep' in 'deep devotion' means strong, but in line 27 Clarke plays with the word 'deep' by using it in a different way. What does it suggest here?
- The last two lines come as a bit of a surprise – but maybe we should expect to be surprised by now. How do the last two lines belong together? How does the poet achieve a final emphasis on 'yours', by using the line before it?

Final thoughts

By this point, you've looked at the way the poet uses repetition, rhyme and sentence forms, and how he plays with words and ideas. Now read the poem again (aloud if you can), enjoying what you've found.

One Flesh by Elizabeth Jennings

Elizabeth Jennings was born in 1926. Much of her early poetry was deeply personal, and the themes of loneliness, change and loss are often still found in her later work.

flotsam floating wreckage, particularly of a ship or its cargo

Read and revise

1 The title is central to the meaning of this poem. It comes from the Bible:
   'Therefore shall a man leave his father and mother, and shall cleave
   unto his wife and they shall be one flesh'.
   Once you know that, almost every word in it has a bearing on the poem.
   - In line 1 which *two* words are exact opposites of 'together'?
     Underline them.
   - The picture presented in this line tells us that the couple are not
     together. What else does it tell us they don't do?

2 The woman seems to be thinking about the past.
   - Which words in line 3 suggest this?
   - If she were back in her childhood again, 'All men' would be
     'elsewhere'. What does this say about her state of mind now, and her
     state of body, too? Think about the title again.

3 What 'new event' could they be waiting for? Think about 'the shadows
   overhead'. What 'shadows' lie ahead for both of them?

4 Look at line 7.
   - Which word suggests that their love has gone?
   - What does 'flotsam' suggest to you?

5 What does 'cool' in line 8 suggest? Where else does this idea of
   coldness occur in the poem?
   - The couple 'hardly ever touch'. How does this remind you of the title?
     Find the other reference to touching. Think about its meaning.

6 Look at line 10. The poem becomes reflective here. What is there in this
   line that makes it seem as if the poet is thinking as she goes along?

7 In the final stanza, some connections are made between the couple.
   - Look at line 13. Which two words in the line are a direct contrast?
     Underline them.
   - Compare this line with line 1 of the poem. Why do you think the poet
     has chosen to make the two lines so similar and yet different?

8 What does the poet liken the silence to? How does she emphasize that
   it doesn't draw them together, even though it connects them?

9 How does the poem become more personal in the last two lines?

10 Look at line 18. Underline the contrasting words. What is their effect?

11 The *rhyme scheme* in the first two stanzas is the same. In the final stanza, though, the rhyme in lines 2 and 4 is repeated in line 6. What effect does this have on the final message of the poem? What words are emphasized by the change in the rhyme scheme?

Final thoughts

Read through the whole poem again. Why do you think the poet chose to end it on the word 'cold'? How has the choice of title affected your understanding of the poem?

Comparing poems

In your English Literature Examination, you will be offered two questions to choose from on each poetry cluster, and some cross-cluster questions – there's some advice about these at the end of the Poetry section. You only have to answer *one* question on poetry, though – any one you like on whichever cluster, or clusters, you've looked at. Whichever question you choose, you'll be asked to compare poems in your answer, usually *three* or *four*, and you'll be told to use at least one *pre-twentieth-century* poem in your answer. The pre-twentieth-century poems are clearly marked in your **Anthology**, and they'll be indicated on the exam paper too.

You might be asked to compare *meanings* in poems, such as the *feelings and attitudes* in them, or the poets' *ideas*, and you'll be asked to compare the *style* of the poems – the way the writers have used *form, language* and *structure* to express meanings. That sounds a bit forbidding, but if you've worked through some of the poems, using the questions in the book, you'll already have a good idea of what this means. You might also be asked to write about some of the differences between *twentieth-century* and *pre-twentieth-century* writing.

Of course, there are a lot of questions which could be asked on each cluster, and any number of combinations and angles you could use in choosing three or four poems to tackle the questions. Here are some examples of the sorts of comparisons you could make between the **Hearts and Partners** poems. There could be lots of others, though – as long as you know the poems well, you should be able to tackle anything. The comparisons are given in note form, as you might do when preparing a response. Remember, you'll need plenty of evidence from the text to support your points.

Meanings

One way to see poems is in men's and women's attitudes to love.
- **The Beggar Woman**: man exploiting gender power, social position.
- **Rapunzstiltskin**: man more romantic, foolish, but same attitude. Women in both poems more intelligent – but helps escape in **Beggar Woman**, leads to death in **Rapunzstiltskin**.
- **Our Love Now**: man thinks damage can be healed, woman not. Woman wants loyalty, commitment, as **Beggar Woman**.
- **To His Coy Mistress**: woman clings to society's rules, man wants to break them, as in **Beggar Woman**.

Another way might be the end of love.
- **One Flesh**: pair grew apart gradually; now 'cold'. Death ahead. Personal poem – writer's parents.
- **Our Love Now**: unlike **One Flesh**, picture of conflict from outside – and dialogue, not reflection. Structure suggests ending of relationship.
- **The Beggar Woman**: ending more upbeat than first two. Woman's victory, message for man to learn.

Style

- **To His Coy Mistress**: poem structured as argument – three stages shown by indentations. Range of imagery – time, love, death. Tone = praise/threat/passion. Tight rhyme and rhythm.
- **i wanna be yours**: like **Mistress**, first person, asking for love. Range of imagery too, but deliberately unusual. Vocabulary simpler, appeal more direct. Lines shorter, but not regular. Some strong rhythms, but not regular. Tone urgent, insistent – repetitions. Less serious in approach.
- **Rapunzstiltskin**: draws on fairy stories – form, language relate to this. Free verse, not tight schemes of first two. Language simple, like the Clarke – mostly modern, but some older language too. Not a romantic poem, despite language – Rapunzel's attitude.

Differences between twentieth- and pre-twentieth-century poems

Several possibilities for different *attitudes* through time:
1 **Beggar Woman** and **Coy Mistress** both show men as instigators of sexual situations – so does **i wanna be yours**, but the man asks; in **Rapunzstiltskin** the woman implies interest.

2 In **Beggar Woman** woman in control, though at end. In **Rapunzstiltskin** (pre-twentieth situation, twentieth point of view), woman has intellectual control, but man has power. In **Our Love Now** woman has upper hand throughout (and last word).

3 **Beggar Woman** = casual encounter for male, not female. In **Our Love Now** both committed to long term, but her commitment absolute. In **Rapunzstiltskin** he initiates, she tries to control, is destroyed.

Comparing *style*:
Language of **i wanna be yours** and **Rapunzstiltskin** more casual than two pre-twentieth-century poems. Sharp contrast in personal pronouns. 'I' not capitalized in **i wanna be** . **Coy Mistress** uses 'thine', 'thy' and 'thou'.

Questions

In your answer to either of these questions you must refer to **both** pre-twentieth-century and twentieth-century poetry.

The pre-twentieth-century texts are **The Beggar Woman** and **To His Coy Mistress**.

Foundation Tier

Love sometimes places people in difficult situations. Write about these situations in **three or four** poems from this section, and about how the poets show the difficulties.

You should write about:
- the nature of the situations
- the attitudes shown towards the problems
- how the poets show the difficulties in the way they write.

Higher Tier

Men and women often think and behave differently in relation to love. Write about **three or four** poems from this section, showing how the poets have presented men's or women's attitudes.

You should write about:
- the attitudes of men or women in the poems
- the way the poets show men's or women's attitudes
- your responses to the poems.

The Pen by Raymond Carver

Raymond Carver (1938–88) was an American poet and writer of short stories who wrote in plain, unadorned language about the lives of ordinary men and women on the margins of society.

Glossary

facilely too easily, superficially

Read and revise

1   A term that will be very useful in thinking about this poem is *personification*. This is when something that isn't human is described as though it is – 'The pen that told the truth' is the first example in the poem.
   - Underline 'that told the truth', and look for other examples of personification.

2   The idea of the pen that 'told the truth' is picked up again in line 10. How does the poet make the connection?
   - Look at the feelings the pen has in lines 8–12. How could these feelings be a writer's feelings? In what circumstances? Look for other examples of where the pen's feelings might be the poet's.

3   Look at what the pen writes the first time, at line 16. How does the line relate to:
   - what has happened to the pen, and why it hasn't been writing?
   - a writer who might be struggling to write?

4   Look at lines 20–7.
   - Underline all the words and phrases in lines 20–5 that suggest that this is the last time the pen will write.
   - Lines 26–7 contain the pen's last words. Can you see anything here that might be anticipating death?
   - It's interesting that the lines written by the pens also use personification ('the damp fields asleep'). Look at the other lines which the pens write, and underline other examples of personification. Why do you think the poet includes these?

5 Look at lines 28–33, which describe the disposal of the pen.
- Again, underline the words that suggest that this is final.
- Is there a suggestion of death here too? Think about how the pen is finally destroyed.

6 Lines 33–7 describe 'another pen'. Find *three* suggestions in lines 35–7 that this pen isn't as good as the last one.

7 Now look at the last two lines – the lines the second pen writes. Line 39 seems to be a warning about 'Darkness'. What do you think it could mean? Darkness often *symbolizes* death. How does it do that here?

Final thoughts

Look back to questions 1 and 2, where you thought about the pen representing, or symbolizing, the poet himself – or his inspiration. Looking at it this way, what happens in the last 11 lines, especially when the pen 'quit working forever'?

The Writer by Sujata Bhatt

Read and revise

1 The first three lines are a simple, direct statement. Look at where line 3 starts. How does this lift the phrase out, so that you notice it? This is an example of how a poet uses form to express meaning.

2 Line 5 is also indented, so that the line stands out. Why do you think 'in your heart' is important?

3 Paper is 'dry, flat'.
- Look through the poem for all the things which aren't dry, and underline them (e.g. 'waterfalls').
- Now look through for things which are the opposite of 'flat' (e.g. 'soil' and 'roots'). When you reach the end of the poem you'll see how 'Paper is dry, flat' is a key line for the *structure* of the whole poem.

4 Lines 8–13 form a question about how the idea can be transferred from inside the poet's head to the page.
- Find the word in the middle of the question that refers to something inside the poet. Mark it, and link it to a similar idea in line 5.
- Find and underline all the references here to the idea of moving a plant, starting with 'soil'. How effective is this image?

5   Nouns are the names of people, places or things. Look through the rest of the poem underlining the nouns. How do the nouns change during the course of the poem? How does the poet show a widening picture of the landscape?

6   At line 26 the poet asks, 'How would things move on paper?'
   - Do you think that she has created a strong sense of movement?
   - Reading from line 15 to the end, find and underline all the verbs, beginning with 'grows'.
   - Think about whether the verbs show strong or weak actions.

7   In lines 22–3, the position of the clouds comes as a surprise.
   - Why might the clouds be described as being beneath the fish? Think about these two possible explanations:
     a it's part of an imaginary landscape, reflecting the 'heart' and the 'spirit'
     b it's the reflection of clouds in the water that's being described. How would this interpretation make sense of line 24? If you think this is right, make a note in the margin.

8   Now look at the last three lines, 27–9.
   - Line 27 marks a change in the poem. Up to now, all the sentences have been statements or questions – but this is a command. Who is being commanded?
   - How is the strength of the tigers shown?

Final thoughts

The tigers' walking 'shreds the paper' – it comes to life, and the poem is destroyed, not written! But you've just read the poem. This is a *paradox* – an apparently contradictory or absurd statement that turns out to be true. Read the poem again, thinking about what the poet is doing. Has she succeeded in saying that writing's impossible? Was she trying to?

'The Time I Discovered Myself to be a Poet' by William McGonagall

William McGonagall was born in Edinburgh in 1830. He wrote topical verse (poems about contemporary events and people) of a uniformly dreadful quality, of which he was nevertheless extremely proud, and performed it in public at every available opportunity. Strangely enough, the fact that his verse is so bad has ensured its survival when the work of many technically better poets has been forgotten.

Read and revise

1 From the first stanza you can see that the poem is supposed to be regular in form.
   - Which lines rhyme at the end? Check through the rest of the poem. Does the poet manage to stick to this?
   - He sets up a rhythm as well. Look at line 2, for instance. If you say it aloud, you should hear three stresses or beats – the same with line 4. How many can you hear in line 3?

2 Stanza two starts off in the same rhythm as the first.
   - What do you make of line 3 this time? What is wrong with it?
   - Compare the last words of each third line in stanzas one and two. There's a natural stress on 'Faith' in stanza one – is there a similar stress in stanza two? What is the effect of this?
   - Now look at the description of what Rev. Gilfillan is doing. Remember that this poem is intended to praise the man. What's wrong with the description of him in the last line of this stanza? Why do you think McGonagall has chosen the unfortunate word 'bawl'? (Look at line 29!)

3 Look at stanza three and think about the meaning.
   - In line 33, is it clear who is in distress?
   - Line 35 has a different problem – the Lord will bless who? 'Him' would complete the sentence – why hasn't he put it in?

4 Stanza four doesn't really improve things.
   - What picture do the words 'lofty head' give us? Do you think that this is what the poet meant?
   - Look at line 38. Do the stresses work here?
   - Can you see any other problems with this stanza?

5 Now read the P.S. In what way is this humorous?

6 Read the poet's introduction again, in the light of what you've learned.
   - Look at the second sentence, which begins 'During the Dundee holiday week'. Read aloud the second, third and fourth phrases in the sentence. What do you notice? Does 'while lonely and sad in my room' fit with any of the ideas here? If not, why might it have been included?
   - What else in his introduction seems a little silly to you? Why should you have responded like this?

Final thoughts

The poet seems very pleased with the introduction to the poem in the *Weekly News* – but perhaps there's something he doesn't realize. *Irony* is 'the use of words to express a meaning which is the opposite of the literal meaning'. What might be ironic in the sentence beginning 'Here is a sample'?

Sonnet 17 by William Shakespeare

Shakespeare probably wrote his Sonnets in the 1590s, although they were not published until 1609. They are written in the first person, and mostly record the poet's intense feelings towards a young and beautiful nobleman who has never been satisfactorily identified.

Glossary

deserts deserved reward
numbers verses
number list
metre system of arranged and measured rhythm in verse

Read and revise

1 The first two lines introduce the theme and set the tone for the poem.
   - What is it that people in the future would have difficulty in believing?
   - Which two words in these lines say how wonderful the poet's beloved is? Underline them.
   - The idea of 'in time to come' starts here. Skim through the poem quickly, underlining all the other words and phrases that refer to time, or the passing of time.

2 In lines 3 and 4 Shakespeare protests that his verse isn't good enough yet. How is it lacking? (Look at line 4.)

3 At line 5 the poet starts imagining how his poem might be received in the future.
   - Which words in line 5 show the beginning of wishing, or imagining?
   - What things are praised in lines 5 and 6? What do you think he means by 'in *fresh* numbers'?

4 Look at lines 7 and 8.
- What is the specific word of praise here? Why would his praise not be believed?
- Shakespeare often uses contrasts and balances within a line. Which two words in line 8 are in direct contrast? Underline them, and mark 'contrast' in the margin.

5 Look at lines 9 and 10.
- Shakespeare is imagining a time in the future. How is this shown in what will have happened physically to his poems?
- What does 'of less truth than tongue' mean? Thinking about it as 'more words than truth' may help.

6 Look at lines 11 and 12.
- 'Rage' may seem an odd choice of word here, but 'rage' can mean 'passion' too – perhaps even a kind of madness. The 'rage' here is an exaggeration – which word in line 12 means 'overdone'?

7 The form of the poem is, as the title tells you, a *sonnet*. Look this up in the **Glossary**. The last two lines are a completion of his thought but also signal a change of tone.
- If you look at the last words of each line, you'll soon work out the *rhyme scheme*. How is the end (the last two lines) a change from this?
- Because lines 13–14 form the only *rhyming couplet* (two consecutive lines that rhyme), and because they're at the end, these two words are really emphasized: 'time' and 'rhyme'. Why has the poet made this very deliberate choice? Look back to the first line, and think what the whole poem has been about.

Final thoughts

Read the poem again, noticing how Shakespeare has combined praise of his lover with thoughts about writing and time.

The Secret by Denise Levertov

Read and revise

1 The poem is structured in two halves. Where does the second half begin?

2 There is great emphasis on words at the ends of lines in this poem. For example, 'discover' at the end of line 1. Discovery is a key idea in the poem. Skim through the rest of the poem, marking all the words that have a similar meaning.

3   A single word on a line by itself obviously stands out – especially if the line has a full stop at the end of it. 'Poetry' (line 4) therefore becomes a strong word. Why has the poet chosen to put weight on this word?
    • The word is emphasized by something else, too. What happens after line 4 that makes you dwell on the word even more?

4   In stanza four, the last line is emphasized in a similar way.
    • Look back over the last two questions and make a note on the page of exactly how 'the secret' is stressed.
    • 'forgotten' (line 15) is used in contrast to 'discover'. In question 2 you looked for all the words that meant 'discovered' – now do the same thing for 'forgotten'.

5   Look at line 18. The line break after 'I love them' might raise the question (in the pause), for what? There's one answer straight away, in the next two lines – but then there are also some others. Find all the other reasons she gives. You'll see that this forms the *structure* of the second half of the poem.

6   Look at line 21.
    • 'loving me' is given emphasis. How?
    • What is the relationship between the poet and the reader here?

7   'Forgetting it' in line 23 comes as a surprise and is emphasized in the usual way. But how does the poet make you wait for the explanation?

8   Look at the stanza beginning at line 25.
    • 'discover it again' a thousand times means they will have done something else a thousand times. What?
    • Look at line 28. Which other line does it remind you of?

9   The most important reason for the poet to 'love them' is stated in lines 33 and 34. The poet stresses its importance in a number of ways.
    • Look at line 32 – it produces the same effect as line 24. (Look back to question 7.)
    • Now look at line 34. What makes the pause at the end of the line feel even longer?

Final thoughts

Read the poem again, noticing how simple and direct it seems to be, and noticing all the pauses you've been aware of. Think about the lack of imagery and the very direct personal statements. What effect do these have?

The Thought-Fox by Ted Hughes

Ted Hughes (1930–98) was born in Yorkshire and went to Cambridge University where he met and married the poet Sylvia Plath. His poetry celebrates the beauty and vitality of the natural world and also its violence. He was Poet Laureate from 1984 until his death in 1998.

Read and revise

1 Line 1 both introduces the idea and establishes the time and the setting.
   - 'I imagine' is the key to the whole poem. What does the poet imagine, and how does it set the scene for what is to follow?
   - The time, too, is important for the atmosphere of the poem. How is the idea of the fox helped by setting the poem at this time of night?

2 In line 3, who is feeling 'loneliness'?
   - How does the description of the page add to the sense of loneliness?
   - Is the poet writing in line 4, or isn't he?

3 Look at stanza two.
   - How is the darkness emphasized here? Find two examples.
   - How 'near' to the poet is the 'something' in line 6? (Remember the beginning of the poem, and the end.)
   - Where exactly does the sense of something happening, something moving, begin? Find the point and mark it.

4 Look at stanza three.
   - Though the words 'black' and 'white' are never actually used in the poem, the two colours are suggested a lot. How are they suggested? Why? (Think about what the poem is describing.)
   - The 'fox' begins to appear here. Which physical features are mentioned, or suggested? (You'll need to read on to line 13.)
   - The 'movement' begun in the last stanza continues here. How does the poet make the touches of the fox's nose into two distinct, delicate movements by the choice of punctuation?
   - In lines 11 and 12 the movement seems to accelerate. How does the poet do this? Look at the choice of punctuation as well as the words, and at the line divisions.

5 Look at stanza four.
   - Think about the colours suggested by the words in line 13 – and notice the word 'neat'. Apart from the movement of the fox, what could 'neat prints' refer to?

- There are several words that describe or suggest movements of different types. Find them and underline them. What is the dominant feeling at the end of this stanza?
- The rhythm in the last line here is steady and strong – is it in the lines before it? How has the poet used the rhythm to emphasize what he means?

6 Look at stanza five.
- Which words here suggest something getting closer, or stronger? Look carefully at each word in lines 17 and 18.
- Which words in this stanza refer to seeing and thinking?

7 Now look at stanza six.
- The fox is made to seem like a very 'animal' thing here, not human at all. How does the poet establish this in the last stanza?
- In the last two lines the scene returns abruptly to the opening. The scene is unchanged, except for one thing. What?
- How does the poet manage to suggest that the page being printed has nothing to do with the writer?

Final thoughts

At the end, the thought seems to be almost independent of the poet, even though it is his. How does line 20 suggest this, as well as the last stanza?

Read the poem again, concentrating on the opening 'imagine', and the way that the *metaphor* Ted Hughes chooses for the thought – a fox – seems to have a strong life of its own.

Comparing poems

For general advice, see **Hearts and Partners**, pages 54–6.

In terms of *meanings*, one way to compare poems would be to think about the difficulty of writing. You could choose to write about **The Thought-Fox**, **Sonnet 17** and **The Writer**. That's three poems, one of which is pre-twentieth-century, so it's a valid choice. The comparisons are given in note form, as you might do when preparing your answer. Remember, you'll need plenty of evidence from the text to support your points.

- In **Thought-Fox** poet wants to write, but cold, late, lonely, blank page. Thought comes, almost independently of poet.
- **The Writer** is a different problem. Plenty of ideas – forest used again. Difficulty of getting on to paper, which is 'dry, flat', the powerful things that live 'in your heart'.

- **Sonnet 17** different again. Has inspiration, can imagine writing it down, perhaps – difficulty with readers of poem. Future readers may not believe the beauty of his beloved, unless he has a child to inherit it.

There are several aspects of *style* that could be compared and contrasted. You could, for instance, look at the writing of **The Secret**, **The Writer**, **Sonnet 17,** and the William McGonagall poem – four poems, two of which are pre-twentieth-century, so you've satisfied the rubric.

- **The Secret** is a very simple poem – free verse, no imagery, but careful line divisions to emphasize meaning.
- **The Writer** a highly-wrought poem, full of imagery. Personification shows strength of poet's ideas – suprising shift at end. Line divisions used carefully – no rhyme, like **The Secret**.
- **Sonnet 17** the opposite. Tight rhyme and rhythm. Not the same volume of imagery as **The Writer,** but tomb image striking.
- McGonagall poem also uses strict rhyme, rhythm (20th / pre-20th difference in this section), but unlike Shakespeare, he fails to stick to it, doesn't use devices to convey meaning.

Questions

In your answer to either of these questions you must refer to both pre-twentieth and twentieth-century poetry.

The pre-twentieth-century texts are **Sonnet 17** and **The Time I Discovered Myself to be a Poet**.

Foundation Tier

What do these poems show about the difficulties of writing? Compare **three or four** of the poems in this section.

You should write about:
- what the difficulties are
- how the poets show the difficulties
- the differences between the poems.

Higher Tier

Did any of the poets in this section write in an interesting way about writing, in your opinion? Compare **three or four** poems from this section.

You should write about:
- interesting things they have to say
- the ways they chose to write
- why you found these poems interesting – or why not!

Life Doesn't Frighten Me by Maya Angelou

Maya Angelou was born in Missouri in 1928. After a turbulent early life she achieved fame as a writer and poet and is now Professor of American Studies at Wake College, N. Carolina. Her poetry is full of good humour, courage and appetite for life.

Read and revise

1   Which of the fears mentioned are specifically children's fears? Identify these by marking them.

2   How does the poet create the child's voice? Apart from what you've found already, identify
   - *vocabulary*
   - attitudes
   - places

   which particularly belong to children.

3   Which of the fears might be particularly a girl's fears, rather than a boy's? Mark these.

4   Now look at the form of the poem.
   - How are the first two stanzas the same? You'll have to look at rhymes and repetitions.
   - There's only one reminder of the first two stanzas in stanza three – what is it? How do the sentences and rhymes here create a child's voice?
   - Stanza four returns to the form of the first two. Stanza five is different, but there's still a line repeated from earlier in the poem. Underline it.
   - Stanza six (lines 33–40) is completely different. Compare the *rhyme scheme* with that of the previous stanzas. How is this one different? Also, there's no repetition from earlier. Why is this? Look at the last four lines. What are they about?

Final thoughts

Read the poem again, noticing how many times the speaker denies being afraid – and at the end she denies it four times in a row! If a child said this to you, would you believe it? Why would they say it?

'The world is a beautiful place'
by Lawrence Ferlinghetti

Lawrence Ferlinghetti, born in 1919, was one of the so-called Beat Generation of American writers and poets who emerged in the 1950s. They rejected the conventional thinking and morality of the time, and their work was characterized by experimental forms and provocative ideas.

Glossary

improprieties unsuitable or indecent behaviour or actions
mortician undertaker
congressional connected to a meeting or conference

Read and revise

1   The appearance of the poem is rather unusual, with short phrases and irregular lines, but running through it is a series of balances. One of the ideas that is 'weighed up' through the poem is time.
    - It begins with 'not always being' in line 4. Underline this phrase, and the other two references to time in lines 1–11. Notice where they fall on the page, too.
    - The last word in line 5 contrasts sharply with the last word in line 6. Which word further on in the section then forms a sharp contrast with 'hell'?

2   The next 'section' runs from line 12 to line 19.
    - The balance between 'good' and 'bad' has altered here – which side is stressed more? Mark the two words which emphasize this.
    - Mark the two phrases in this section which are about time. How does the layout of the lines help to stress these balances?

3   Look at lines 20–9.
    - Look at lines 23 and 24. What sort of people are being blamed here for some of the 'bad' things that happen?
    - Death is suggested again in lines 25–7. Which direction does it come from? Mark the word that indicates this. How does this connect with line 24?

4   Now read lines 29–39 to the end of this section.
    - What is the poet saying about society by calling it a 'Name Brand' society (line 29)?

- Lines 31–7 list some of the people in society who are the cause of the 'improprieties'. Pick any group of these people and try to decide why the poet might think about them this way. Why are priests likened to 'patrolmen'?
- Notice how the poem keeps its flow by linking sounds together. What's the sound link between 'distinction' and 'extinction'? And between 'priests' and 'patrolmen'? And what's repeated three times in lines 35–7?
- 'The thousand natural shocks/That flesh is heir to' is a quotation from Shakespeare's play, **Hamlet,** when Hamlet is also thinking about life and death. Which word in line 38 tells you the poet's attitude to human beings?

5 The next 'section' also runs for 20 lines, from 40 to 59.
- Look at the balance of 'good' and 'bad' in these lines. Which has a very strong edge here?
- The lines almost seem to 'dance' along here. (Which word is on a line of its own?) It's done with repetitions again. Look for the number of words which end with 'ing'. What do most of these words describe? Look for the number of times the word 'and' is used. What effect does this have?
- Line 59 sums the whole section up. How?

6 Line 60 seems to be starting a new section. How does it do this? Compare the start of the previous section. Here, though, instead of starting a new section, everything is brought to a halt, in form and in thought. How does the poet produce this effect? What's missing?

7 The balance between 'good' and 'bad' is going to take one final twist – which word in line 61 tells you this?
- The last two words in the poem form a contrast. In what way? Who has the final say?
- The word 'mortician' is placed in the middle of the line, almost as though it's holding the poem up. Which phrase (also deliberately in the middle of the line) a few lines above does the idea of a 'mortician' directly contrast with?

Final thoughts

Read through the poem again, appreciating the balances between one thing and another, and the way the poet uses the placing of the lines and sounds to link ideas together.

Elegy for Himself by Chidiock Tichborne

> Chidiock Tichborne wrote this poem the night before he was executed for his
> involvement in a plot to assassinate Elizabeth I in 1586. He was only 28 years old.

Glossary

tares weeds
a shade a ghost; unreal

Read and revise

1   Look at stanza one.
    - The poem begins with Tichborne's central feeling that he is in his 'prime of youth'. What ought he to be feeling about his life, instead of the 'frost of cares' that he feels it has been? What does frost do?
    - Look at line 2. Underline the two words in the line which are opposites. The line works through a *metaphor*. What does he compare his 'joy' with?
    - Now look at line 3. Underline the word which suggests good things, or richness, and the word which suggests the opposite, and then look at the whole comparison in the line.

2   The poet makes us feel his despair by saying the same thing over and over, in different ways. The form of the poem helps us feel this by using a lot of repetitions.
    - How are lines 1–3 the same? Which words are repeated?
    - Work out the rhyme scheme in stanza one (which last words rhyme?). Now look down the other two stanzas – the rhyme scheme is repeated. Which line is identical in each stanza? What effect does the repetition have?

3   Each fifth line in the poem is a *paradox* (see **Glossary,** page 110). In stanza one, how is the poet's 'day' past? What is his life being compared with?

4   Look at stanza two. Pick out all the contrasts.
    - Which line do you think is at the heart of the poet's feelings?
    - In what way has the poet not been 'seen' yet?
    - Look at line 11. How is his 'thread' about to be cut? In what way isn't his thread completely 'spun' or finished yet?

5 Now look at stanza three. It has a growing sense of despair, and things coming to an end.
   - The poet has already suggested that his life is ending prematurely. According to line 13, when did his death begin?
   - Look at line 17. Think about the first 'glass' as referring to a wine glass – what's that saying about his life? Think about the second 'glass' as referring to an hourglass. If his 'glass' is 'run' (out), what is that saying about his life?

6 How does the poet deliberately reinforce the sense of repetition in this last stanza? Look at line 16, and think how it prepares for the last line of the poem.

Final thoughts

There isn't much progression of thought here in this poem – it's almost like one statement, repeated over and over. Why has the poet done this? Read it through again, noticing all the repetitions of thought and form.

Vitaï Lampada by Henry Newbolt

Sir Henry Newbolt (1862–1938) was a lawyer as well as a poet, who is now best remembered for writing stirring patriotic ballads like Drake's Drum.

Glossary

Vitaï Lampada the title means 'the beacon of life'
Gatling an early type of machine-gun
smote past tense of 'smite', to hit hard

Read and revise

1 Look at stanza one.
   - Line 1 starts to establish the situation. Where is the poem set? Which words are used to tell the reader that the situation is a tense one? Underline them.
   - In the lines 2–4, what are the difficulties that are being faced? Notice the way that the poet repeats the word 'and' to make the difficulties seem to mount up.

2 Lines 5 and 6 are about motives – why you have to do your best even if the odds are stacked against you.
- What might 'a ribboned coat' be in school? What might it refer to in adult life?
- 'a season's fame' is about the game – but about life too. What sort of rewards are unimportant?
- What is the key word in line 6, do you think, that sums up the poet's attitude to such fame? Underline it.

3 Stanza two moves to another situation.
- Where is this stanza set? Why is the sand 'sodden red', do you think? What is the 'square' that has broken? (Think about defensive formations in the army.)
- Just as in the first stanza, there's a list of difficulties. What are they here? Notice the use of 'and' again.
- How is England 'far', and why is this another difficulty?

4 • 'Honour' is 'a name' – just a word, that doesn't mean anything. Which word in line 15 tells you that this isn't the way to think about it? Look back to the first stanza – the *structure* is the same. What does this tell you about the message of the poem?

5 Now look at stanza three.
- This stanza draws everything together. How does the language of line 17 tell you this?
- What are the words (the final line of each stanza) compared to? How is this comparison continued into line 23? Who are 'the host behind', do you think?

Final thoughts

The poet clearly approves of the attitude he is describing. Read the poem again, looking for the words that tell you this. The structure helps here, too, by repeating the same line at the end of each stanza, and then ending the whole poem with it.

Now think about the title of the poem. What is 'the beacon of life'?

Song of the Worms by Margaret Atwood

Margaret Atwood is a Canadian poet and novelist, and is one of the leading female writers of her generation.

metaphysic system of thought focusing on the causes of things

Read and revise

1 Read through the whole poem. What do you make of the first line? Which words imply that the worms are ready to hit back?

2 Look at line 3.
   • What does 'one' imply about the worms' purpose?

3 Look at line 4. What does this tell us about the worms? Do you think they really *are* worms?

4 Look at lines 7 and 8.
   • Which words in line 7 suggest freedom? Underline them.
   • Which words in line 8 suggest that this freedom is secret?
   • What is the only freedom they have? Why isn't this enough?

5 Look at lines 9–16.
   • What is the attitude of the 'boots' to the worms' loving? Underline the word that tells you.
   • Lines 11 and 12 give the worms' viewpoint. What is being done to the worms, that they know this angle of the boots so well?
   • Lines 13 and 14 are about how the boots work, and think. What do you understand by 'kicks and ladders'?
   • Lines 15 and 16 tell us the feelings of the worms. Why are they 'afraid' of the boots? If you think about the boots as a method of control, who do you think might be represented by the 'foot' in line 16? What do the worms feel about this 'foot'?

6 Lines 17–21 mark the shift in the poem, and the beginning of the 'message'.
   • Line 17 begins with 'Soon'. How does this relate back to the first line of the poem? Look quickly through the rest of the poem to the end, and mark the other words that refer to time. How is 'soon' a threat?
   • Look back at the verb forms in the first 8 lines of the poem. Notice that they are all passive. Now underline all the verbs in lines 17–21. What is different about all these verbs? Which ones are to do with war, and which with destruction?
   • Which word is repeated in lines 17 and 19 (it's part of the verb)? What does it show about the worms' attitude now?

7 In the context of the poem, what does 'there will be no more boots' mean?

8 In line 25, 'your' comes as a surprise.
   - So far, the opposing force to 'we' has been described impersonally, as 'the boot' and 'the foot'. Now it's described with a personal word. How is this a threat? Who is being threatened?
9 The change in tone is made even sharper by line 26.
   - Which word in the line suggests a human speaker, not an animal?
   - How is the word 'Attack' made stronger? Look at it on the page!
10 How does the last line seem menacing?

Final thoughts

Maragaret Atwood is best known as a feminist writer. Her poem could be about any group of people, or about repression generally. How might you interpret 'Song of the Worms' as being about the position of women? Think about the details of the poem. Can you think of any other groups of people that the poem might apply to? There are a number of alternative interpretations.

Light Shining Out of Darkness
by William Cowper

William Cowper (1731–1800) was a rector's son who suffered all his life from periods of severe depression; many of his poems reflect the sense of man's isolation and helplessness which was one of the symptoms of his condition. The collection containing this famous hymn was published in 1769.

Glossary

grace help given by God
providence power guiding human destiny
err make a mistake

Read and revise

1 God is praised in this poem for his strength and power.
   - What specific actions are described in the first stanza?
   - Quickly skim through the rest of the poem, looking for and marking other words and phrases which praise the nature of God.
   - Is there anything 'dark' here? Think about line 4. Who controls the darkness?

2   Read stanza two, which shows God at work.
  • Think about the title again. What could we think of as dark here? Which word means 'light'?

3   Stanza three deals with the human race for the first time.
  • What do the saints need that God can give (line 9)? Which other two words, in lines 9 and 10, show that they are weak and afraid?
  • What do the threatening clouds actually contain?
  • What do you understand by the clouds 'shall break'? Think about rain and also about clouds parting. Which image do you prefer? Think about the image in the title as well.

4   Look at stanza four. Which word in line 13 implies again that humanity is weak?
  • Which two words (one in line 15, one in line 16) contrast directly with each other? What does this say about the nature of God?
  • How does the idea presented by the two contrasting words connect with the title again? Think back to the choice you had to make about 'clouds' and 'break'. Which interpretation do you prefer?

5   Look at stanza five.
  • Underline all the words which refer to plants or flowers.
  • Which two words in lines 19 and 20 contrast directly with each other? What does this say about what happens to people in their lives, and the nature of God?

6   The final stanza stresses again human weakness and God's power.
  • What do the first two lines suggest about humanity?
  • Human beings cannot 'scan [God's] work' and make sense of it. According to the last two lines, who can?

Final thoughts

The poem is made to seem very simple and plain. How does the form help it to do this?

Comparing poems

For general advice, see **Hearts and Partners**, pages 54–6.

In terms of *meanings*, there are a number of ways these poems, or some of them, could be compared and contrasted. You could look, for instance, at how three or four poems are about *the way people deal with fear*. The poems you could look at might be **Life Doesn't Frighten me**, **Elegy for**

Himself, and **Vitaï Lampada** – that's three, and one of them is pre-twentieth-century, so you've followed the instructions. The comparisons are given in note form, as you might do when preparing your answer. Remember, you'll need plenty of evidence from the text to support your points.

- **Life Doesn't Frighten Me**: from child's viewpoint. Fears childish. Poet pretends to 'smile' at dangers– repetition makes reader believe she *is* afraid.
- **Elegy for Himself**: danger real, not imaginary – execution. Poet young – cannot laugh off fears. Depressed by his fate. Only afraid of one thing, unlike girl in **Life Doesn't Frighten Me**.
- **Vitaï Lampada** about learning to deal with fears and dangers. First two poems about individuals – here about behaviour as part of team. Face danger 'with a joyful mind' – unlike **Elegy**. Learned when young, carry into later life, leave behind – not in first two, again. Death as glorious, but not selfish. First two poems about 'I' – this doesn't appear in **Vitaï Lampada**.

In terms of *style*, there is a wide range of poetic style and technique to think about. Let's suppose you had chosen to write about **The world is a beautiful place**, **Elegy for Himself**, and **Vitaï Lampada**. Three poems, one pre-twentieth-century, so that's fine. What might you write about?

- **The world is a beautiful place**: irregular lines, unlike others. Meaning conveyed through positions of words/contrasts/sound links. Structure through repeated lines/lists/repeated words. Mood humorous, cynical.
- **Elegy for Himself**: no humour, depressive. Regular lines and verses – thought doesn't develop, unlike **The world**. Repetition of words, phrases, sentences, lines.
- **Vitaï Lampada**: uses imagery, like **Elegy**, but unlike **The world**. Mood, joyful, determined, unlike others, and no cynicism or humour. Repetitions, though, and lists with 'and's', like **The world**, though effect different.

Questions

In your answer to either of these questions you must refer to both pre-twentieth- and twentieth-century poetry.

The pre-twentieth-century texts are **Vitaï Lampada** and **Light Shining Out of Darkness**.

Foundation Tier

Several of these poems are about fear. Compare the way that **three** or **four** poems deal with fear.

You should write about:
- the fears that are shown
- the way people respond to fear
- how the poets show people's feelings, by the way they write
- differences between the poems.

Higher Tier

There are several different attitudes to facing difficulties shown in the poems in this section. Compare **three** or **four** of the poems.

You should write about:
- some of the difficulties shown in the poems
- the way people deal with them
- how the poets show the difficulties
- differences between the poems.

Catrin by Gillian Clarke

> Gillian Clarke was born and brought up in Cardiff and is one of the best-known Welsh poets writing today. Much of her poetry reflects her strong sense of national and cultural identity. She now lives in a remote cottage in west Wales, where she earns her living as a freelance writer and teacher.

Read and revise

1   The first line establishes a number of important things about the poem.
   - There are two people involved in the poem. Which personal pronouns are used to identify them here?
   - Which word in the line establishes the relationship between the two?

2   Look at lines 6–10.
   - Find and mark the line which repeats almost exactly the first line.
   - In this line, 'I' and 'you' are almost like opposites. Which word gives us the first idea that the two are joined together in some way?
   - Find other words in these lines which suggest togetherness, and words which suggest conflict – and the one word which says how they feel about each other.
   - These words suggest two people who are joined closely together, but still fight. What physical thing are they joined by?

3   Find and mark the three descriptions of the place where the action is set.
   - 'White', 'blank', 'glass tank'. What is this room, and how do these descriptions show how the speaker feels about it?
   - Look at line 10. There are two other words here which make the room seem impersonal. What are they?
   - Look at lines 11–14. How does the speaker 'colour' the walls? Look carefully at what she 'writes' and colours with.

4   Look at lines 14–17.
   - Which words are about, or imply, conflict?
   - Which words or phrases suggest being apart?
   - What does 'ourselves' imply? What is there in the way the poem is set out that suggests that the poet wants you to think about this word?

5 Lines 18–20 mark a change in the poem.
- Line 18 is still in the past tense – but how do we know that the poet is looking back on the events described in the first section?
- The real shift is clear at the end of line 20. What indication is there about the time that the events described between here and the end of the poem are taking place? Which word tells you this?
- Which word in the line tells you that nothing has changed? Underline it.

6 There's still conflict between the two. Find and mark the words in lines 20–9 which suggest conflict.

7 Look at the description of the daughter in lines 22–4.
- What does the mother admire about her daughter?
- Look at the words she chooses – and listen to them. Which sounds are repeated. What effect does the repetition have?

8 When the mother looks at the daughter, and listens to her request, 'that old rope' is brought up from 'the heart's pool'.
- What is the rope? It's not physical rope here.
- It's an 'old' rope now. Dating back to when?
- The rope is first described as a 'tight' rope, and here it is 'Tightening about my life'. Why is it 'tight', do you think? Will it ever let go?

9 The feeling is brought on by the look on the girl's face, but also by her simple request. Why should this bring out 'love and conflict', do you think?

Final thoughts

Read the poem through again, taking in all the ideas about love and conflict. You might like to think about one more detail – the first thing Gillian Clarke describes. She watches 'people and cars taking/Turn at the traffic lights'. Why did she choose to include this detail in this short poem about mother and daughter, do you think? The 'rope' is red, too – maybe for more than just one reason. Think about what this might link up with.

A Parental Ode to My Son, Aged Three Years and Five Months by Thomas Hood

Thomas Hood (1799–1845) was the son of a London bookseller. He was a friend of many of the famous literary figures of nineteenth-century London and is best known for his humorous and satirical verse. His son Tom, the subject of this poem, was born in 1835.

Read and revise

1 Stanza one introduces both the content and the style of the poem.
   - What is the difference between the mood of the boy described in line 1, and what he's doing in line 2?
   - What does the father's reaction to his son in line 2 suggest about his feelings towards the boy, at this point? Contrast this with his feeling about the boy in the last stanza!
   - Both the statements in line 7 are likely to prove wrong, because of what happens in line 8. How?

2 Some of the humour comes from the way the poet has used the form – the *rhymes* and the arrangement of the lines.
   - In lines 11 and 12, when the father thinks of the child as he 'wings the air', what is he actually about to do?
   - The poet makes this humorous, not simply by putting the two things next to each other in consecutive lines, but also by linking them together in another way. How does he do this? Look at the last words of the lines.
   - In line 17, unusually, the poet starts the brackets halfway through the line. Why do you think he does this?

3 Look at stanza three.
   - Line 21 describes the boy's play as 'harmless'. How is this contradicted in the next line?
   - How is 'ever sunny' in line 25 contradicted?

4 Look at stanza four.
   - The father uses 'dove' in line 31 as a *symbol* of peace. How do the boy's actions in line 32 deny this? Identify other examples of contradictions throughout the poem.
   - Look at lines 37–8. How is 'dawning life' contradicted – possibly! – by the next line? How does the rhyme help to strengthen this?

5 Now look at the final stanza.
   - Line 51 describes the boy 'breathing music like the South'. How does the boy make the father breathe (line 52), and why?
   - There's a *paradox* in the last line. Who does the father really want to write about? What must happen before he can write about him?

Final thoughts

Try reading the poem again, ignoring all the words in brackets, and look at the words and images the father would like to associate with his son. How are they romantic and ideal? Now read it again with the brackets!

Upon My Son Samuel his Going for England, Novem. 6, 1657 by Ann Bradstreet

Ann Bradstreet was born in England but emigrated to America in 1630. She is highly regarded both as an early woman writer and as the first American poet.

Read and revise

1 This simple poem takes the form of a prayer, but within it the poet cleverly uses her chosen form to stress her feelings about her son.
   - The second word of the poem is 'mighty'. Skim through the poem quickly, looking for examples of the power of God.
   - Which two lines in the poem say exactly what the mother wants God to do for her son?

2 Line 4 might confuse the modern reader, because a word is used in a different sense from modern use. 'I stay'd for' here means 'I waited for'.
   - How does this explain line 3?
   - How does this make the child more precious?

3 Look at lines 5 and 6.
   - The child was a precious gift – which makes giving him back a big thing to do. Look at the last three words of line 5 and line 6. The second is *almost* a repetition of the first. Why do you think the poet has chosen to do this?

4 Look at line 7. The giving of the child is underlined by the balance of power shown through the rhythm and rhyme of the line. Which two words within the line rhyme? This is called internal rhyme. These words are direct contrasts. What effect does this have?

5   Look at line 10. If you haven't already spotted this when you responded to question 1, how is God's power shown here?

6   God has the power to 'preserve' the boy, or not. What other power does he have, according to line 13?

7   Look at line 16. Read it carefully. How does the rhythm change here? When a poet uses a regular rhythm, it's usually the irregularities that are important – they make us notice something because it's different. Why has the poet chosen to interrupt the flow here with an extra word? Underline it, and make a note in the margin about the change in rhythm.

8   In line 17, 'If otherwise I go to rest' means 'If I die without seeing him again'. If this does happen, what does the mother hope for after her death? (See lines 19 and 20.)

Final thoughts

Read the poem once more, noticing how much the child is at the centre of the mother's thoughts.

Lullaby by Rosemary Norman

Read and revise

1   Look at the first three lines.
   - The first three words form a command. Quickly skim through the poem, noticing and underlining other similar commands.
   - After reading the title, what is surprising about the first few lines? How does the poet emphasize the surprise by use of commas?

2   In the next three lines (4–6), how do you know that the child is a little older? Underline the verbs. Where are they placed? How does this stress the mother's fears?

3   What age do you think the child is in lines 7–10? Think about the movements involved.

4   Look through the next 16 lines, down to 'my girlfriend pregnant'.
   - Identify all the different stages here, as the poet sketches the child's progress.
   - How does the poet show, in lines 25 and 26, that the lullaby could relate to any child – that it's not just written as though it's one specific boy or girl saying this?

5 Two more stages of adult life are mentioned in lines 27–31.
   - Which of a mother's fears about a grown-up child are shown here?
   - Why do you think alternatives are being shown here, by the use of slashes?
   - What is completely new about the stage being suggested in lines 30 and 31? (Where is the child?)

6 Look at lines 32–3.
   - How does the poet prepare the reader for the surprise in the last line? Think about the length of line 32.
   - Think about what the last line might mean. In one sense, it takes us back to the beginning – how? It's also *ironic* – what has the child been telling the mother to do throughout the poem?
   - Perhaps there's another meaning, too. A baby needs milk from its mother. What might a grown-up child need? 'Milk' wouldn't be literal, if we read it this way – it would represent something the mother has to give.

Final thoughts

Read the poem through once more, identifying all the mother's fears. A lullaby is a soothing song. How might the mother be soothed by this song? The poem shows the mother's attitude by looking at her from the child's point of view.

Nettles by Vernon Scannell

Vernon Scannell was born in Lincolnshire in 1922 and his first collection of poems was published in 1948. Much of his poetry combines everyday language and domestic subjects with a sense of lurking menace.

Read and revise

1 The first line establishes what has happened, clearly and quickly. Several things about the way the poet has chosen his words make it seem simple.
   - The form of the sentence is simple. Where is the subject? Where is the verb?
   - Where does the sentence end? (This is called an end-stopped line.)
   - The first line is factual. Which word in the second line shows the father starting to reflect on what has happened? Underline it.

2   In the second line, the writer uses a *metaphor* which he continues to use throughout the poem.
    • What is this and why is it an appropriate idea? (Think of what the nettles have done.)
    • Which word in line 3 continues the comparison?
    • The nettles are personified – made to seem human. Which word in line 3 gives them human motives?

3   In line 6, what do the blisters on the boy's skin look like? Underline the word that tells you.

4   In line 11, which word makes use of *personification* again? Underline it.
    • What does this word, and 'regiment' in line 3, imply about numbers?
    • What does the same word imply about the way the nettles move?

5   Which words in line 13 suggest that the nettles are treated like humans?

6   Look at line 15.
    • The 'busy sun and rain' are personified – what is it that they can do?
    • Which two words in the line use the military comparison again?
    • What does 'tall' suggest about the rate of growth? How is this threatening?

7   There's a threatening force at work – what is it? Think about lines 14 and 15 again.

8   Now look at the last line.
    • What else is growing up, apart from the nettles?
    • The poet has chosen to make this the last line of the poem – but he could have placed this idea earlier in the poem. Does it make a difference that it's held back until now?

Final thoughts

In the poem, the father takes action against the force which has hurt his son – but the last line tells us that he can't protect his son all the time. Because it's the last thought, and comes after the idea that nature has more nasty surprises in store, what else could it be about? There's more than one way of interpreting this line. Read the poem again with this in mind.

For Heidi with Blue Hair by Fleur Adcock

Fleur Adcock was born in New Zealand in 1934 and has lived in England since 1963. Her poetry is often subversive and ironic in tone – as with this example.

Read and revise

1 The poet creates a number of voices in the poem. Look at stanza two.
   - In lines 6–10, it's the headmistress's voice we're hearing. Which words or phrases are chosen because they sound like 'school teacher speak'?
   - What do you think the headmistress means by 'apart from anything else'?

2 Look at stanza three.
   - Why does the father stand up for Heidi?
   - One of the elements in the poem is humour. Line 10 itself has an element of humour – how does the poet build on this at the end of the next stanza (line 15)? What else does line 15 tell you about Heidi?

3 In lines 13–17 we hear the father's voice. He's defending his daughter. Can you say anything else about him as a parent, from what he says?

4 Lines 17–20 give us Heidi's voice. What do you make of her attitude?

5 The mention of the mother's death comes as a surprise to the reader.
   - Why do you think the poet introduces this into the poem? Does it make you feel differently about Heidi? Does it explain anything about her, or about her father?
   - The poet says that the mother's death 'shimmered behind the arguments'. What do you think this means?

6 Line 25 says that the teachers 'twittered'. What do you think this means? What does it imply?
   - If the teachers are being criticized in some way, who is doing it?

7 Now look at stanza six.
   - 'An act of solidarity' is part of the humour, because it has two meanings. Who could the friend be showing solidarity for as well as for Heidi? Think about the colours. Which interpretation do you think is better?
   - How is the battle 'already won'?

Final thoughts

At the end of the poem, we still don't know who the speaker is. If it's the poet, writing about something she witnessed, what is her relationship with the people involved? We don't know from the poem, but we do know whose side she's on in the 'battle'. Read through the poem again, trying to work out how we know who she supports.

Comparing poems

For general advice, see **Hearts and Partners**, pages 54–6.

In terms of *meanings*, these poems are all about relations between parents and children, in some way, but they examine several different aspects. You could choose to look at poems which show parents protecting children, for instance, and look at **Upon My Son Samuel, Catrin, Lullaby** and **Nettles**. You'd be looking at four poems, one of which is pre-twentieth-century, so your choice meets the requirements. The comparisons are given in note form, as you might do when preparing your answer but you'll also need plenty of evidence from the text to support your points.

- **Upon My Son Samuel his Going for England** shows desire to protect child. Mother prays for him – willing to give child to God. If she dies, only wishes to see him happy after death.
- **Catrin** not as simple. Mother again wants to protect child from danger – but relationship here (from birth) is of conflict as well as love – daughter 'defiant', mother is 'fighting you off'.
- **Lullaby** is a reversal. Child aware of dangers mother wants to protect it from – assures the mother everything will be all right. Child will protect itself. First two about particular parents and children – this is universal.
- **Nettles** about a father and son – others about mothers. Child has been hurt – parent has failed to protect, and despite attacking nettles, will be unable to protect the son in the future.

In terms of *style*, you could look at **A Parental Ode to My Son, Upon My Son Samuel**, and **Catrin**. Three poems, two of which are pre-twentieth-century, so it's OK.

- **Parental Ode** has two moods and corresponding styles. Father's ode ·uses romantic/idealistic vocabulary and imagery, with archaic words and images from nature. Father's spoken words in brackets more direct, sharp, creating humour.
- **Upon My Son Samuel** is serious – language of prayer, desperate, addressed to God. Some language natural, but mostly formal, and regular rhyme and rhythm schemes, varied cleverly for effect.
- **Catrin** different from other two. No rhyme scheme, regular use of rhythm – poem relies on central image, 'that old rope', and others, and on sound links. Changes in tense and perspective used too. A serious poem.

Questions

In your answer to either of these questions you must refer to both pre-twentieth- and twentieth-century poetry.

The pre-twentieth-century texts are **Upon My Son Samuel his Going for England, Novem. 6, 1657** and **A Parental Ode to My Son Aged Three Years and Five Months**.

Foundation Tier

Several of these poems show tensions between parents and children. Compare the way that **three** or **four** poems in the section do this.

You should write about:
- the tensions in the poems
- how the characters in the poems deal with the tensions
- how the poets show the tensions by the way they write
- the differences between the poems.

Higher Tier

Several of these poems show strong feelings, from parents or children, or both. Compare the way that strong feelings are presented in **three** or **four** of these poems.

Balance Sheet by John Montague

Read and revise

1   Look at 'Loss' (page 92). Find the word in the first line of each stanza that refers to an action, and underline it. Now look at all the underlined words together. What kind of picture emerges?

2   Each stanza focuses on an aspect of life that has been lost. Look at stanzas one to five.
   • Identify the type of life mentioned in each stanza. Make notes at the side of the page.
   • Look for words in each stanza that suggest:
   a the freedom or abundance of the natural world
   b the resistance of nature to order and regimentation.

3   Look at stanza six.
   • Which words in line 22 suggest imagination? What is going to happen to imagination from now on?
   • How does the last line shift the focus towards the second half of the poem?

4   Now look at 'Gain' (page 93).
   • The poet deliberately underplays the 'gains' throughout this section. Why do you think he does this?
   • Look at the first three stanzas in this section. How is each of the 'gains' made to seem small and limited? Look at numbers, time and place.

5   Look at the last 'Item' in stanza four.
   • Which words here remind you of the items in the 'Loss' column? Look at the language, as well as at what has happened.
   • How does the idea of an 'unobstructed view' (line 39) bring the reader back to stanza six of 'Loss'? Why does the poet do this?
   • How might the living be 'quick enough to come straight in'? (It helps if you know that 'quick' also means 'alive'.)

6 Look at the form of the 'Loss' and 'Gain' sections.

- Count the items on each side. What do you learn from this?
- How does the regular form of 'Loss' change in 'Gain'? Why do you think the poet has chosen to do this?

7 Lines 43–51 show a change in language, form and structure.

- The form of the 'Items' has deteriorated gradually throughout the 'Gain' section. What happens here? Look at the position of the lines on the page. What effect does this have?
- The change in language is surprising. Balancing gains and losses is usually seen as an impersonal business activity – something done by bookkeepers and accountants. Find all the personal words in this stanza and underline them.
- The final stanza adds a third element to the structure, too – it isn't just Loss/Gain. What would you call this part?

Final thoughts

The poet does not say directly whether the building of the road is a loss or a gain overall – but he certainly makes his feelings clear. Read through the poem again, noticing how he influences the reader by his choice of words.

Irony is the name given to a deliberate choice of words that say one thing but mean exactly the opposite. How is 'Gain' ironic in the end?

In Romney Marsh by John Davidson

Read and revise

1 The first stanza establishes the framework of the poem.

- Images of sight and sound run right through the poem. Find and underline the two key words in this stanza that establish this.
- The rhythm of the poem is also established in this stanza. Read it aloud (or 'hear' the lines in your head), exaggerating the natural rhythm of the lines. You should hear four beats in each line. Which words do they fall on?
- Look at lines 2 and 3. Where does the first beat fall in each line? Underline the words.

2 Colour is a central feature of the poem.

- Which colours are mentioned in stanza three? Underline them.
- The colours are given vitality by their association with active verbs. Find the verbs and underline them. Which verbs also reinforce the sense of movement?

3 Look at stanza four.
  - Pick out the words which signify movement, colour and sound. What effect do these words produce?
  - The rhythm changes for the first time in this stanza. Look at line 13. Which part of the line doesn't fit the rhythm of the rest? Which word in particular stands out?

4 Look at lines 19–20.
  - When you say these lines, which sounds are repeated? (Repetition of initial consonants is called *alliteration* and use of the same consonants or vowel sounds within words is called *assonance*. See **Glossary**.)
  - The rhythm in line 20, like that of line 13, is different from the rest. Which word is thrown into focus by this change?
  - Now put these technical devices together. How has the poet used sound links and a change in rhythm to suggest what is actually happening to the sky?

5 Look line 23. Which part of this line is different in rhythm? What does this make you notice?

6 Look at the last stanza.
  - Which word reminds you that it is now night?
  - How does the poet make the beach seem like a huge musical instrument?
  - Look again for the changes in rhythm. In which lines do they occur.

7 Rise and fall in movement is closely linked with sound. Look at the rhymes in the poem. Notice how many of them are associated with high and low sounds – for example, the rhymes in lines 5–8. See if you can find similar examples in the rest of the poem.

Final thoughts

It is the linking of colour, movement and sound that bring this poem to life. Read through the poem again carefully, looking for examples of this.

A Major Road for Romney Marsh
by U. A. Fanthorpe

U. A. Fanthorpe taught English for many years, and also worked for a time as a hospital receptionist, before having her first poems published when she was almost fifty. Her work is characterized by wit and humour blended with compassion.

Read and revise

1   Look at lines 1–2. How does the poet suggest that this place is special and different?

2   Look at line 3.
   - This line suggests that the place is ready for change. What is there about lines 1–2 to suggest that change is both unnecessary and undesirable?
   - Lines 1–2 are both complete short sentences. How is line 3 different?

3   Look at line 4.
   - Which letter sounds are repeated? (Repetition of initial consonants is called alliteration.)
   - Repetition of sounds links things together. What else links the three items in this line, apart from the sound of the words?

4   Now look at lines 5–6.
   - Notice how one of the sounds in line 4 is picked up again in line 6, linking the whole picture together.
   - How in line 6 does the poet convey a sense of the scale of the place? Has the same idea been suggested before? (Look back at line 1.)

5   The 'Major Road' of the title is referred to in lines 7–8.
   - What features of roads are mentioned here?
   - How does the poet make them sound threatening?
   - A feature of some of the language of the poem is abbreviation of words. Where is this first shown in these lines?

6   Look at lines 9–11.
   - The poet uses *personification* to give life and individuality to the trees and churches in these lines. How does she do this? (Look up personification in the **Glossary**.)
   - Which words suggest isolation?
   - Which words suggest that this can be a difficult place?

7   Look carefully at the language of lines 12–13. What else do you notice, apart from abbreviations? In what ways are the words becoming more compressed?

8 Look at lines 17–18.
- 'It wants . . .' is repeated here for the third time. Is there anything in the description of the place to suggest that it either wants or needs any of the things mentioned?
- How does the poet make line 18 seem almost nonsensical? Why might she want the reader to think this is nonsense?

9 All the words in the last line are contracted – the vowels have been left out. Do you find this line threatening or merely silly? Give reasons for your answer.

10 Two opposing points of view are offered in this poem.
- How does the poet express each point of view, apart from the choice of language? Think about positioning on the page and the use of punctuation.
- The brackets might make the words to the right seem less important, which would suit the poet's point of view. But which side has the last word? What is the significance of this?

Final thoughts

The poet leaves the reader in no doubt about her view of the **Major Road for Romney Marsh**. Read the poem again, noticing all the ways she has let you know what she thinks.

Composed upon Westminster Bridge, September 3, 1802 by William Wordsworth

William Wordsworth (1770–1850) was born in Cumbria and educated in the Lake District, to which he remained deeply attached all his life. His influence on English poetry was revolutionary in its rejection of 'heroic' themes and 'poetic' language in favour of everyday subject-matter expressed in the language of normal speech – things which we take for granted today.

Read and revise

1 Line 1 states emphatically that nothing on earth could be lovelier than this view of London at sunrise. Skim through the poem and find other words which praise the city. Start with 'so touching' in line 3.

2 Look at lines 2–3.

- What does the poet think should be 'touched' by such a beautiful sight?
- How does he stress the 'dullness' – i.e. insensitivity – of someone who does not stop to look? Look at the position of 'Dull' in the line and in the sentence.

3 The 'sight' (line 3), stressed by the rhythm, is the central focus of the poem – it is all about what the poet *sees*. Again, skim quickly through the poem, noting how often Wordsworth refers to things you can see or to their appearance.

4 In what ways might 'the beauty of the morning' be 'like a garment' (lines 4–5)?

5 Look at lines 5–8.

- Which words suggest the city is exposed? Underline them and note how they are emphasized by their position in the lines.
- Which word in line 8 echoes the vowel sound in the 'lie/sky' rhyme in lines 6–7? What effect does this have?

6 Lines 1–8 describe the scene and lines 9–14 focus on the poet's response to it. How is this change marked? Think about the *rhyme scheme*.

7 The first word in line 9 is 'Never'. Where is this word picked up again? Why do you think the poet repeats it so quickly?

8 Line 10 contains a list.

- Look back through the poem and find an earlier list. Compare the two lists. What is the difference between them?
- Look at the thought in lines 9–10 and then look back at the first line of the poem. If you stress the first word, what is the poet saying about the city?

9 Line 11 continues the emphasis on sight and seeing. What does the poet do, apart from see?

10 'A calm so deep' (line 11) is one of the features of this place at this time that the poet loves. Find and underline all the other references to calm or quiet, or the words that suggest calm.

11 In lines 12–14, the poet makes the city seem like a living thing by personifying it. 'The river glideth at his own sweet will' (line 12) is an example of personification – the river, being inanimate, cannot have a will of its own.

- Find and underline all the other words that make the city seem alive. How effective are they?

12 What is the effect of ending the poem on two exclamations? (Look at the punctuation.)

Final thoughts

Read the poem again, looking at all the ways in which Wordsworth expresses his wonder at this view of London.

Glasgow 5 March 1971 by Edwin Morgan

Edwin Morgan is a Scottish poet and translator who has published several volumes of poetry, some of it experimental like The Loch Ness Monster's Song and some, such as Glasgow Sonnets, starkly descriptive of Scottish urban landscape.

Read and revise

1 This poem is one of a series called 'Instamatics' – each one describes a snapshot, a moment frozen in time. Look at lines 1–4. What has happened just before the photo was taken?

2 The 'ragged diamond/of shattered plate glass (lines 1–2) describes the shape of the broken glass but makes us think of the precious stone, too. Apart from its value, what quality is diamond best known for? Is its colour cold or warm?

3 Look at the description of the young man's face and the girl's leg (lines 5–10).
   • Underline the verbs in lines 6–7. Why has the poet chosen not to describe what is actually happening? What is the effect of this?
   • Find and underline the active verb in line 9. Which word in the same line seems medical rather than dramatic? What adjectives might the poet have chosen if he had wished to dramatize the blood?
   • What would you normally connect with blood in conjunction with a white coat? How does this reinforce the idea suggested by the use of 'arterial' in line 9?

4 What connection can you find between the 'wet-look' coat (line 10) and the image in line 11?

5 In lines 13–14 the reactions of the two young people are briefly touched on. How does the poet present them? Is there any sense of drama or pain? How might the poet have dramatized the situation if he had wished?

6 Look at lines 15–16.
   - What do you notice about the verb in line 15?
   - In line 16, how does the poet make the young men's actions seem detached and clinical?

7 Look at line 19.
   - Do we expect the youths' faces to show expression? If so, what kind?
   - Line 19 is end-stopped, which means that it is a self-contained unit of sense which finishes at the end of the line and is marked by a pause. How else is this line made to seem simple and unadorned? Look at the shape of the sentence – the *syntax*, or word order – and the shape of the sentence in lines 20–1.

8 Look at lines 22–3.
   - The poet has distanced the reader emotionally from the action throughout. In what way are these lines an appropriate conclusion?
   - Why do you think the drivers pretend not to have seen the incident?

9 Now look back at the title of the poem. If the poet had wished to write a dramatic account of this incident, what title might he have chosen? What is the effect of the title he did choose?

Final thoughts

When you look at the poem as a whole, there is very little imagery and no strong use of rhyme or rhythm. Sentences are simple, and full stops always come at the ends of lines. Taken in conjunction with everything else you have noticed, how does the way the poet describes the incident condition your response to it?

Read through the poem again with this, and the effect of the title, in mind.

Ninetieth Birthday by R. S. Thomas

R. S. Thomas is a Welsh clergyman and poet who has spent his working life in isolated and often poor rural communities. This, together with the Welsh landscape, has been the primary influence on his poetry.

Glossary

nightjar night bird with a whirring call
buttressed propped up (buttresses support the outer walls of buildings)
abyss an immeasurably deep gulf

Read and revise

1 Look at lines 1–2. What is the first word in the poem to suggest distance? Underline it.

2 The poet ends line 2 with 'walked' and begins line 3 with 'On slow foot'.
   - What effect does the natural pause here have on the pace of the poem?
   - What does 'On slow foot' suggest about the track?
   Note how these two features work together.

3 Read quickly through lines 1–14. Note how many of the breaks between one unit of sense and the next happen in the middle of a line.
   - What is the effect of this on the pace of the poem?
   - How does it convey the 'feel' of the journey up the track?

4 Lichen is a primitive, slow-growing plant. In what other ways is the passage of time suggested in lines 3–4?

5 The natural world beyond the track is described in the sentence that begins in line 5 and runs on to line 11.
   - Quickly find and underline the names of all the plants and creatures mentioned.
   - The poet makes things vivid by using personification. Find the words which produce this effect – there are several, beginning with 'yield' (line 6).

6 How does the poet emphasize the sense of stillness and quiet in lines 8–11?

7 Look at lines 11–14, which emphasize the steepness of the hill and the distance from the rest of the world.
   - How is the steepness shown? (Remember the person walking up the track!)
   - The 'signal' (line 13) is the sun flashing on the sea. How does this suggest the distance the person has travelled?
   - How does line 14 suggest height and remoteness – and perhaps a sense of moving into a different world?

8 What is the effect of the gap between lines 14 and 15? (Look back at the end of line 14.)

9 Why is the village 'lost' to the old woman? Why does it exist 'in her memory only' (line 20)?

10 Look at line 23.
   - How is time personified here?
   - What do you think is meant by the 'knife shaving the bone'?

11 Look at lines 24–7.

- How do these lines stress the gulf, in time and distance, between the old woman's world and the visitor's?
- How does the last line remind you that the old woman lives in the past?

Final thoughts

The poem appears to suggest that the old woman, whose ninetieth birthday is the occasion of this visit, is far removed from the modern world to which the *narrator* belongs. As the narrator climbs the hill, he gets further away from his starting point in distance and in time. Read the poem through again, noticing particularly the effects of the phrases at the ends of lines.

Comparing poems

For general advice, see **Hearts and Partners**, pages 54–6.

In terms of *meanings* these poems are all about places at particular times. There are a number of ways of looking at them. If you are asked about poems that deal with the beauty of places, for instance, you could write about **Composed upon Westminster Bridge**, **In Romney Marsh**, and **A Major Road for Romney Marsh**. You'd be looking at three poems, two of which are pre-twentieth-century, so your choice would meet the requirements.

Here are some suggestions, in note form, of the sort of things you might write.

- **Westminster Bridge**: the beauty of the city – morning – bright colours – stillness – water quiet.
- **In Romney Marsh**: sight/sound of seaside – afternoon, changing to evening – colour changes – movement – beach/waves.
- **A Major Road for Romney Marsh**: same place, different point of view. Wind, as in **In Romney Marsh**; solitude, as in **Upon Westminster Bridge**; but intrusion of the modern world on the place. The pre-twentieth-century poems show unqualified admiration of nature; the twentieth-century poem has a sense of intrusion and loss.

In terms of contrasting *style*, you could look at how the poets convey their views in **Balance Sheet**, **A Major Road for Romney Marsh**, **Glasgow 5 March 1971**, and **In Romney Marsh**. You'd be looking at four poems, two of which are pre-twentieth-century and two twentieth-century, so your choice would meet the requirements.

- **Balance Sheet**: one side of argument given, then the other, with a third, personal section at the end. Poet's view conveyed by irony.
- **A Major Road for Romney Marsh**: poet uses two sides of the page, alternately, to offer two 'sides'. Brackets, abbreviations, used to convey attitude, and the threat of change.
- **Glasgow 5 March 1971**: view conveyed by distancing, coldness, lack of imagery, simple syntax.
- **In Romney Marsh**: the opposite of **Glasgow** – highly wrought, intense use of sight and sound, strong rhythm, use of imagery and personification.

Questions

In your answer to either of these questions you must refer to both pre-twentieth- and twentieth-century poetry.

The pre-twentieth-century texts are **In Romney Marsh** and **Composed upon Westminster Bridge**.

Foundation Tier

In several of the poems in **Time and Place** the poets express a view of the places they describe. Compare the way that **three** or **four** of the poets express their views.

You should write about:
- what the poets say about the places
- how they say it
- differences between the poems.

Higher Tier

How is time important in these poems?

You should write about:
- the time of day in the poems
- when the poems were written
- how the poems are written
- differences between the poems.

At the end of the questions on the groups of poems in the **Anthology,** there will be three further questions which ask you to compare poems from different groups. You could choose to respond to one of these instead of a question on an individual group. The question numbers will be 38, 39 and 40. Questions 38 and 39 compare particular groups and question 40 allows you to choose any poems from the Literature **Anthology**. The questions will probably be very similar at Foundation and Higher Tier. Below are examples of the sort of questions that might appear here. You will still have to refer to at least **one** pre-twentieth-century poem in your answer.

Question 38: Many of the poems in **Hearts and Partners** and **That Old Rope** deal with close relationships. Compare the way that different poets show relationships. Choose **two** poems from **Hearts and Partners** and **two** poems from **That Old Rope**.

Question 39: Many of the poems in **When the Going Gets Tough** and **Time and Place** convey strong attitudes. Compare the way that different poets convey their attitudes. Choose **two** poems from **When the Going Gets Tough** and **two** poems from **Time and Place**.

Question 40: Some poems are interesting for what they say, and some for the way they say it. Sometimes it's both! Compare **three** or **four** poems from the Literature **Anthology** which you found interesting, giving your reasons, and saying which of the categories they fit into.

When you set about responding to a question in the examination, it's important to take some time to plan your work. In this section there's an example of a model answer plan to a particular question. But remember that there could be a number of other ways to plan a successful response.

Suppose that the question you were going to tackle in the exam was this one, on **Time and Place**:

Foundation Tier

In several of the poems in **Time and Place** the poets express a view of the places they describe. Compare the way that **three** or **four** of the poets express their views.

You should write about:
- what the poets say about places
- how they say it
- differences between the poems.

You could choose **Balance Sheet**, **A Major Road for Romney Marsh**, **Composed Upon Westminster Bridge**, and **In Romney Marsh**. There are two pre-twentieth-century poems here, and two twentieth-century ones, so that meets the requirements.

Here are some notes which suggest how you might plan your answer.
- **Balance Sheet/Major Road**. Both attack a coming change which may destroy a beautiful, remote, rural environment. Both environments are peaceable, isolated; **Balance Sheet** about a place which is full of natural life rather than bare like **In Romney Marsh**, but both threatened by new roads. *Style* is similar in some ways – two sides or views shown separately. Point of view developed by *irony*. 'Gains' not really gains – 'it wants', but it doesn't. But **Balance Sheet** has third part. **A Major Road** uses truncated words, capitals, brackets.
- **Composed upon Westminster Bridge** is different – no irony, but honest praise. No threat to environment – written 200 years ago. Praise, not attack. Like **Balance Sheet**, uses rhyme, but more regularly – form traditional and regular, able to use for division of thought. Like **A Major Road**, uses *personification*, but to show London as strong, beautiful body, not as 'small', truculent', 'obstinate'.

- **In Romney Marsh** takes straight view (like **Westminster Bridge**) of scene – unlike Fanthorpe's view of the same place. Uses sight, like **Westminster Bridge**, but strong on sound too. Both pre-twentieth-century poems use regular *rhyme* and *rhythm schemes*, varying them for effect, whereas the twentieth-century poems use rhyme and rhythm more sparingly, loosely, and have more critical views.

In this section you will find three responses to the Higher Tier sample question which follows the story **Flight** by Doris Lessing. The writers were all Year 10 students preparing for the examination. Their work was marked by a Senior Examiner and graded A, C and E respectively. The examiner's comments, showing why these grades were awarded, follow the answers themselves.

The question was:

In **Flight**, Doris Lessing uses pigeons to represent something else. Write about how she does this, and how the author of **one** other story in the **Anthology** uses the same technique.

You should write about:

- the things the authors have used, and what they represent
- why the authors have chosen to use these particular things
- how the authors show that these things are meant to represent something else
- what the authors gain from using this technique.

William

In the stories 'Flight' and 'Your Shoes', the writers express many ideas through the objects in them (pigeons in 'Flight' and white training shoes in 'Your Shoes'). These objects enhance the stories' plots and enable the writers to bring out the history and surroundings of the main characters.

In 'Flight' the pigeon represents the granddaughter Alice; we see a comparison between the two in the way the light shines off them:

'The sunlight broke on their grey breasts.'

'Her hair fell down her back in a wave of sunlight.'

These lines show us how the sunlight is used to link the granddaughter with the pigeon. The linkage shows us the way the pigeons are used to express how the granddaughter has grown up and is now leaving home.

In 'Your Shoes', the trainers could represent two people in the story, the daughter who has run away or the narrator's mother. The daughter is joined with the trainers in their whiteness, for white symbolises purity and cleanliness (which is why it is worn for weddings to symbolise virginity in the bride) because the narrator is wishing to cleanse her daughter through the shoes. This is because her daughter is no longer a member of the virgin club and so has had sex which her mother, the narrator, was trying to protect her from. She may also wish to purify her daughter through the trainers, for in the story it is mentioned that the daughter may have to take up prostitution so that she can feed herself, and the narrator of course does not want this for her special young innocent little girl. The mother may also be trying to mould her daughter through the trainers for they are everything she wants them to be, well presented, clean and, most of all, white (a virgin again) and the mother desperately wants this for her daughter.

The trainers could represent the grandmother due to the fact that they are a comfortable, well-fitting shoe and the grandmother always used to wear shoes that were the wrong size and had a high heel to them:
'Rows of high heels, all of them too small for her.'
The comparison comes in the contrast between these shoes and the trainers and how the grandmother's shoes are so tight, causing corns and bunions, whereas the white trainers are so light and easy to walk in. When the narrator is talking about her mother she calls her a tart, referring to the way she used to dress and act, which makes her like the daughter, and the narrator makes the same comparison:
'My mother was like you.'
This line seems to sum up how the mother/narrator thinks of both her relatives, and so links all three (the white trainers, the daughter and the grandmother) together.

In 'Flight', Lessing shows the pigeons as a symbol of Alice by contrasting one image against another, for example:
'A young pigeon, the light gleaming on its breast.'
This image, along with one of Alice walking up the street with Steve with the light glowing from her face shows us the similarities of the two again with a good use of light.

The trainers in 'Your Shoes' are showing us the mother's need for order in the way she continually moves them around the daughter's room, always keeping them neatly displayed together. The mother's need for order probably comes from her strict and non-truant upbringing as a child, which could also have led to her becoming a school teacher due to her need of order portrayed to her by her parents which came due to their strict upbringing. In this factor the mother feels guilty due to her not bringing her child up correctly, and we can see this in the way she sucks on and cradles the shoes. In this she could be looking for a way of trying to explore the bonding that comes through breast feeding, which the mother had been and the daughter not, and so the narrator is looking for that bond between mother and daughter. She is also trying to make her daughter into a baby again so that she cannot make any decisions for herself and completely relies on her again. On the other hand the narrator could just be demented and rocking for comfort like a baby does but, whichever way you look at it, she is trying to draw comfort from somewhere.

In 'Flight', the writer Lessing gets the idea of growing up across to her readers through the ideas of Alice being the last of many and the grandfather wishing to hold on to her so that he can protect her again. A similar thing is happening in 'Your Shoes' – the writer through the relationship between the three ladies and the shoes is venturing into the ideas of teenage life and the relationships that a child needs with all his or her relatives. In both stories the writers thicken and enhance their plots through using the symbols, for they can explore ideas that would not be possible without them. For example, in 'Your Shoes' and 'Flight' both symbols are attached to movement – the homing pigeon can fly and you use trainers to walk, both viable means of getting away from your parents and elders. This is portraying the need to spread your wings and get away when you are older; both are in different situations but both are the same.

Commentary

William's response to the question begins very directly, identifying the symbols in the two stories quickly and focusing on the writers' purposes. The identification of the pigeon with the granddaughter is made succinctly, with two well-chosen quotations for illustration, and an explanation. William then offers two readings of the shoes in Michèle Roberts's story, exploring the choice of white as a colour for the shoes because of its associations, and anchoring this firmly in the text. Exploration and development, which are the hallmark of this response, are evident in the language here: '*The trainers could represent. . .*', '*She may also wish to purify her daughter through . . .*'. The possibilities of the choice of whiteness are closely explored and analysed before William moves to consider the shoes as symbols for the grandmother, for different reasons.

One of the Assessment Objectives refers to comparisons 'within and between texts', and William compares effectively the two types of shoe in the story, and the people they represent, illustrating this with '*My mother was like you*'. He then builds this – '*This line seems to sum up how. . .*' – into a sensitive insight into the author's purposes and methods.

William then compares this multiple use of imagery by Roberts with Lessing's use – '*by contrasting one image against another*' – and analyses a detail of presentation in Lessing's '*good use of light*'.

Returning to **Your Shoes** – the story he is clearly more interested in – William embarks on a sensitive and close interpretation of some of the meanings expressed by the shoes and how the mother treats them. Even after a convincing view is offered, William gives another interpretation which is equally arguable in context, and then makes a clear evaluation of what can be said: '*On the other hand, the narrator could just be demented and rocking for comfort like a baby does but, whichever way you look at it, she is trying to draw comfort from somewhere.*' William then compares the way the two writers convey '*the idea of growing up*' to their readers through the symbols they use, recognizing the centrality of the symbols in the design and effect of the stories – a convincing response to the final prompt. He gives a further analytical example of this in the ways that '*both symbols are attached to movement*'.

This is a most impressive and enthusiastic response, offering a wide range of interpretations while remaining firmly rooted in the text, and analysing writers' choices, methods and purposes effectively. Much more is written about **Your Shoes** than **Flight**, perhaps reflecting the range of possibilities which the candidate sees, but this does not reduce the mark. This response deserves a mark in the A* band.

Anthony

In 'Flight' the symbol is the pigeons and because they leave and fly away they represent the old man's granddaughter, but as the pigeons will be coming back he realises that she also will. At first he doesn't want to lose either his granddaughter or his pigeons, 'He deliberately held out his wrist for the bird to take flight, and caught it again at the moment it spread its wings.' He wants the bird to feel freedom and realises it is his to give or take. With the granddaughter he just wants her to stay at home with him permanently. In 'Your Shoes' by Michèle Roberts the symbols are shoes. When the writer is clearing out her mother's clothes she noticed that the shoes were badly misshapen, 'all of them moulded to the shape of her poor feet'. So on the way home from there she bought her daughter a pair of new shoes, 'white trainers, you see I know what you like'. The writer thinks she knows her daughter and by buying the shoes is trying to mould her how she would like her daughter to be.

In 'Flight' the writer has chosen to use the pigeons as a symbol because they fly away but do come back. She uses pigeons because they always come back, as the old man wants the granddaughter to do. In 'Your Shoes' the writer uses the new shoes because they have not been worn and are pure, as the person telling the story would like her daughter to be. The phrase 'moulded to the shape' shows that mother of the person telling the story tried to mould herself as the narrator is trying to mould her daughter.

In 'Flight' the writer shows the pigeons are symbols because the old man does not want the birds to go, 'clenched in the pain of loss', as he does not want his granddaughter to go. Eventually he says 'Now you can go' which is referring to his favourite pigeon, but also to his granddaughter, whom he is letting go and marry the postmaster's son. In 'Your Shoes' the writer shows the shoes as being symbols because at the end of the story the narrator is holding them to her breast and holding close to her, while rocking them like her 'mother never rocked me'. The text also says 'Let me hold you while you cry', which shows the narrator thinking of the shoes as her baby.

In 'Flight' the author uses the pigeons as they are easier to show going and coming back than humans. The author also compares the two with nature: 'her long legs repeated the angle of the frangipani stems' and 'the light gleaming on its breast'. In 'Your Shoes' the author gains from using shoes as a symbol because the narrator's mother tried to mould herself to her shoes, as the narrator is trying to mould the daughter as she would like her to be.

Commentary

Anthony begins by locating the device of the pigeons in **Flight** and explaining how they represent the granddaughter. He interprets the symbol in terms of the pigeon's desire for freedom and the old man's power over it, which he wants to exercise over the girl too, and carefully supports a comment with a relevant quotation. Shoes are identified as the symbol in **Your Shoes**, and he implies that they represent the daughter, though this is not clearly explained.

Anthony has chosen to use the prompts as a structure for his response, and now moves on to the reasons that these things have been chosen. A convincing reason is given for each choice, though neither adds much to what is said about the symbols in the first paragraph. However the connection between the narrator's mother and her own relationship with her daughter is more explicitly linked to the idea of being '*moulded to the shape*'.

The way Doris Lessing shows that the pigeon represents the girl is explained well, with two effective references to the text. The use of the shoes is shown too, with some sense of development, '*the text also says . . .*' beginning a comment about '*the narrator thinking of the shoes as her baby*'.

Anthony closes with two convincing suggestions of the '*gains*' of using the pigeon in **Flight**, both of which break new ground, though the comment on **Your Shoes** is a repetition from earlier. Overall, the use of the prompts as structure perhaps held Anthony back a little, producing repetition where more material could have been explored. There is sustained focus on the task, though, effective use of textual details to support argument, and features of the authors' methods explained, and explored a little. A mark well up in the C band is justified.

Lily

In the story 'Flight' Doris Lessing uses pigeons which represent the old man's granddaughter. He uses the pigeons to remind him of his granddaughter who he still treats as if she is still a little girl. She wants to move away and have a life of her own, but the grandfather doesn't want to let her go as she is his last granddaughter that hasn't left. He finds it hard that she is leaving so he threatens to tell her mum; he will be probably thinking that she is going to give in to him but she doesn't care. The granddaughter says that she will always come back to visit, just as the pigeons do when they fly - they always come back to the place they call home. When the old man is holding the pigeon in his hand, and is going to let the pigeon free, he catches it as soon as it is going to take flight; this shows that he wants to let go of his granddaughter but he can't, she means too much to him.

In the story 'Your Shoes' Michèle Roberts uses a pair of shoes which represents the mother's daughter. The mother treats the shoes as if they were the daughter; she holds them close to her and has them sitting beside each other, she has even tied the shoe laces together so they won't get separated or lost and washed and ironed the laces so they are perfect. The mother wants her daughter to be like the shoes, pure and a virgin. The pigeons are used to represent the granddaughter as they fly away and come back, and so will the granddaughter. In both stories they don't want their daughters to grow up too fast.

Commentary

Lily begins her response by locating the feature she has been asked about in **Flight** – 'Doris Lessing uses pigeons which represent the old man's granddaughter'. She then explains why Alice wants to leave, and why her grandfather wants to keep her. She really just tells a bit of the story here, though with a purpose, as she reminds the reader by writing about Alice coming back 'just as the pigeons do'. She then generalizes about the old man's feelings, referring to the details of his behaviour with the pigeon.

Dealing with **Your Shoes**, she again locates the symbol, and identifies it by referring to the details of the way the mother behaves with the shoes. There's explanation here, too: 'The mother wants her daughter to be like the shoes, pure and a virgin', and an explanation of a reason for using the pigeons. Lily ends with a simple comment about a similarity between the stories.

This response does not fit neatly into a mark band. There are flashes of clear explanation of devices in the texts, which would suggest a mark in C, but the response is brief and, even within its length, lapses into narrative. There's some awareness of authors at work, though implicitly, some generalizations, and some use of text. The best fit is in the E band, though the flashes of higher skills push it to the top of that band.

Glossary

The following technical words are used in some of the questions about individual stories or poems.

alliteration the deliberate repetition of initial consonant sounds to gain a particular effect.

assonance the deliberate repetition of vowel sounds or consonants within words to gain a particular effect.

irony the use of words to express something other than the literal meaning – usually the opposite, in fact.

metaphor an image which makes an implied comparison by stating that something *is* the thing it resembles, e.g. 'The icicles were glittering diamonds in the sun'.

narrator the person or voice who is telling the story.

paradox an apparently contradictory statement which is actually true.

personification a device whereby an abstract concept or non-living thing is represented as having human characteristics, e.g. 'Old Father Time'.

rhyme scheme the way rhymes within a poem are organized.

rhyming couplets two lines following one another which rhyme.

sonnet a poem of fourteen lines, usually ending with a rhyming couplet.

stanza a division of a poem in which the lines are arranged in a pattern of metre and rhyme, usually recurring.

structure how the author has organized his work. In poetry, this may simply mean the stanza, though it will reflect the progression of thought too; in prose fiction, it is how the author has shaped his story.

symbol something used to stand for or represent something else.

syntax grammatical arrangement of words.

vocabulary simply the words used!